# A MEDICAL SAFARI

# A MEDICAL SAFARI

Richard Evans

ATHENA PRESS
LONDON

A MEDICAL SAFARI
Copyright © Richard Evans 2006

All Rights Reserved

No part of this book may be reproduced in any form
by photocopying or by any electronic or mechanical means,
including information storage and retrieval systems,
without permission in writing from both the copyright
owner and the publisher of this book.

ISBN 1 84401 748 6

First Published 2006 by
ATHENA PRESS
Queen's House, 2 Holly Road
Twickenham TW1 4EG
United Kingdom

Printed for Athena Press

# *Acknowledgements*

I would like to thank my wife for encouraging me to commit all these experiences to paper. Jill was not with me on any part of this Safari, but over the last twenty-five years has patiently listened to these anecdotes on more than one occasion. I am most grateful to her for all her suggestions and constructive advice on each chapter as it was written.

Karen worked with Jill for many years and her flair as an illustrator is self-evident. My thanks also to Donna Sheehan for her enthusiastic design of the cover and to Lynda at the Land Rover Archive Library for permission to use the cover photograph.

I would also like to thank Thomas Mathew and the staff at Athena Press for their patient support and Rachael March for her efficient help in typing the manuscript.

# Chapter One

The young woman on the operating table in front of me was probably just out of her teens and had arrived soon after midnight on a makeshift stretcher, carried for twenty miles over dusty tracks and rutted roads by her husband, her father and her uncle. She had left her small toddler at her home village with her mother; this first child had been born by Caesarean section after a long and painful labour at the nearby government hospital in Masaka. With this pregnancy Immaculata wanted to have her baby at home, and realising that her time was right, she had taken local medicine at dawn the previous morning to stimulate her uterus to contract. The medicine had worked well and by midday Immaculata's waters had broken and she was having strong, regular contractions. As night fell at her home on the equator the contractions became very intense and painful and she had started to bleed in increasing amounts. The family decided that Immaculata was becoming exhausted and took the decision to carry her to the nearest hospital. After the four-hour journey the little party was met by Sister Ita, the matron of the mission hospital at Kitovu, just outside the town of Masaka; she quickly assessed that Immaculata was in obstructed labour and took blood samples from her and her family before moving the collapsed young mother into the operating theatre suite and sending for me.

As I examined this young woman I realised that she was quickly going into a state of shock; her pulse was weak and her blood pressure barely recordable; her uterus seemed to be 'standing on its head' in a continuous contraction and there was an ominous trickle of blood spreading between her legs. I listened for the baby's heartbeat but found it to be very faint. And then, in the skin crease of her lower abdomen, I saw the scar of her previous Caesarean operation and I realised that this young woman's uterus had probably ruptured. Sister Ita was busy preparing the anaesthetic machine so I told her of my fears and asked her if she could organise some blood in a hurry; we had only ten to fifteen minutes in which to deliver the baby and then start on a repair or a removal of the uterus. Joseph, the laboratory technician, was already establishing Immaculata's blood group and he was then going to take a pint of blood from each of the three relatives who had carried her to the hospital.

With difficulty I found a vein in Immaculata's arm and set up an infusion. I then administered a sleep dose of pentothal and a few seconds later gave her a muscle-relaxing injection so that I could pass a tube into her trachea. This was then connected to the anaesthetic machine and Damiano, the theatre auxiliary, took over the anaesthetic while I went off to scrub up. Meanwhile Sister Ita had prepared the skin and placed sterile towels over Immaculata to leave just her lower abdomen visible. Cutting through the old scar and then separating the muscles I could already see the dark colour of damaged tissue underneath, and on reaching the uterus blood welled up into the wound. The uterus had split transversely right through the site of the previous Caesarean scar and an arm was protruding through this defect. Sliding my hand into the distal part of her now very thin uterus I eased my fingers over the baby's head to bring it up into the wound and I was then able to deliver the baby.

We had a limp baby, but at least there was a heartbeat, and as I set about stopping the haemorrhage from Immaculata's uterus with some carefully placed catgut sutures into the shredded muscle fragments of the torn uterus, Damiano directed his resuscitation skills towards her little son. With the skin closed the operation was finally over, and Sister Ita and I took hold of Immaculata's other arm to set up a second infusion line; with more time in hand I cleaned the skin over her wrist with a spirit swab for a few seconds. I looked at the dark grey swab for a moment. Sister Ita whispered a little aside to me:

'And they say it doesn't come off.'

With three units of blood to be given, the young mother was able to leave the operating theatre and be nursed in a side ward, with her relatives in attendance. It was to be another twenty-four hours before she came around from the shock of this event and realised that she had a baby boy, thanks to her family's decision to make the difficult journey at night. Had they waited until the next morning neither Immaculata nor her baby would have survived.

Rupture of the uterus is now a very rare event in Britain, but in my preparation for work in East Africa I had been trained to cope with such a crisis, from both the anaesthetic and surgical aspects. The shock to my system was that Immaculata was brought to Kitovu Hospital that night, within a fortnight of the start of my two-year tour there. As I walked back to our bungalow, under a clear starlit African sky, I was grateful for the outcome of this first real challenge and realised that it was in no small part due to the superb organisation of Sister Ita and her staff in the various departments of the hospital.

My first sight of the African continent two weeks previously had been from the small window of a Comet as we flew into Cairo Airport in the midday glare of a September day in 1969. As we flew over the machine-gun posts and slit trenches that lined the runway we were aware of the heightened tension between Egypt and Israel at that time and we knew that our two-hour stopover here would not be an easy experience, especially with two small children.

I was on my way to take up a position as medical officer at Kitovu Hospital near Masaka in Uganda. There would be 100 beds in four wards at the hospital, which was run, funded and administered by the Medical Missionaries of Mary, based at Drogheda in Ireland. Our small family was to live and work there for two years. So it was that we found ourselves on this Comet, chartered from BOAC (Better on a Camel) by RAPTIM (Romana Associatio Pro Transvehendis Itinerantibus Missionariis), on a jet plane full of nuns and priests. We were all en route for Entebbe on the northern shores of Lake Victoria, and from here most of the passengers would take onward connections to the various countries of East and Central Africa, but the refuelling stop in Cairo had to be endured. With no sight of any drinks or refreshments in the hot, dusty transit lounge – and only one toilet, the hygiene of which was a matter of immediate speculation – Claire and Jonathan immediately became fractious. The situation was saved by a young priest who pulled a plastic snake from his cotton jacket pocket and with deft fingers brought it to life over the children and their hand luggage. He was returning to his mission station in Zambia after his first home leave in Limerick and had the prospect of a further wait at Entebbe for his continuing flight. His snake-charming skills made our time in Cairo much more tolerable and we finally touched down at Entebbe at 11 p.m. local time.

As we climbed down the steps from the aircraft we were immediately struck by the darkness of the night; even the surrounds of this international airport had no light industry or street lighting and the stars shone out brightly from the black night sky. A tropical storm had just passed through so there was the warm moist smell of recent rain on tarmac, and we walked happily through the scattered puddles into the Arrivals area. Once through immigration formalities we were met by Sister Ita, the Mother Superior of the community at Kitovu, a very slim, diminutive figure in a white habit with a short grey veil. Her warm smile of welcome immediately put the children at ease and we were led out to the hospital estate car and driven to a hotel in Kampala, where we were accommodated for the night in a large family room. My wife had worked as a teacher in Uganda for a year after finishing her Arts degree – what we would now call a 'gap year' – but this was my very first experience of working abroad and in the tropics.

Early the next morning Sister Ita arrived at the hotel to drive me back to Entebbe and the Ministry of Health, where she had arranged an appointment for me to be entered onto the medical register of Uganda. At that time an application in person had to be made with the original documents of all degrees and postgraduate diplomas, so Sister Ita's forethought and planning paid dividends. Within five minutes we were on the way back to Kampala to meet up with the family, who had enjoyed a more leisurely breakfast, and I was officially permitted to practise medicine in Uganda.

Uganda in 1969 was a relatively prosperous and stable country, in the African context, and that part of the country around the shores of Lake Victoria was fertile with a reliable rainfall. The cash crops in this area were coffee and sugar, with the large tea estates in Toro to the north-east. The local staples were plantain, (green) bananas and groundnuts, and the Baganda people who dominated the area around the shores of Lake Victoria were cultured and courteous. Their king (the Kabaka) had recently sought refuge in London, having encountered many difficulties with the then president, Milton Obote, but most of the Baganda Royal Family had remained in the country. The political party which supported the Kabaka was even represented in the government, and a newspaper with royalist sympathies was published weekly, so there was a good degree of tolerance by Obote. Masaka lay ninety miles to the south-west of Kampala and represented an important administrative centre within a sizeable town.

This much I knew as we left Kampala soon after midday, with Joseph driving the Peugeot estate and Sister Ita in the passenger seat half leaning around and drawing our attention to the smart houses in the suburbs of the capital city that soon gave way to shanty towns. Here was a profusion of roadside shops (*dhukas*), and the occasional barber cutting hair under the shade of a mango tree. The all-important watch and clock repairer sat at a small workbench – often on the other side of the tree – his every action through the eyeglass being watched by the timepiece's owner.

As we cleared the last of these settlements, groups of people had gathered trying to cadge lifts from lorries and cars to Masaka and Mbarara, often with their piles of luggage, but Joseph gave them a dismissive wave as we passed and soon we were in the country. The good quality tarmac road passed by dense banana plantations and fields of beans, groundnuts and other crops standing proud in the red soil, but with banked-up earth around the margins of these small fields to prevent any heavy rain washing away the plants. Every so often we would pass by the buildings of a school or a mission and before long we reached the halfway stage of the journey, where the road snaked through a huge papyrus swamp. The two-metre-high reeds stood impressively on either side of the road and small boys would run out to try and generate some interest in the large black catfish which they had caught. Months later I did stop the car on a return journey from Kampala and bought one of these shiny black fish with long barbels, having been assured that they were good to eat. The fish was presented in a semicircle with a tough banana fibre tied around the tail and through the angle of the jaw on one side. The drive home took the best part of an hour and the fish lay on the draining board for another couple of hours, arousing great interest from the cat, before I decided to gut and fillet the purchase. As I cut the banana fibre holding the jaw to the tail the fish leapt to life and thrashed around the kitchen floor until I found something heavy enough with which to stun it; the cat was not seen again for a very long time and the next morning the houseboy chuckled when I regaled him with my mistake.

'These marsh fish can live out of water for many hours, even for a day or two, Doctor, but at least we know it is fresh and good to eat.'

Two hours after leaving Kampala, just as we entered the outskirts of Masaka, we turned off left up a dirt road that led to Kitovu. The cathedral and schools, plus a seminary, were about two miles from the main road, whilst the hospital was another mile further on up a fairly steep hill. Both here and later in Tanzania I was to work in a fine hospital on the top of a hill, and knowing that the majority of my patients would be approaching the hospital on foot I often questioned the wisdom of the people who had chosen the location. Here at Kitovu the picture of the verdant green hilltop in the late afternoon sun, with its spectacular views over to Lake Victoria, was magical. As we stepped out of the car, the light breeze caught by the top of the hill combined with the altitude to give a wonderful climate; we had crossed the equator just thirty miles out of Kampala and yet Masaka had one of the most pleasant climates imaginable.

The hospital at Kitovu was fairly new and in spite of the ravages of the red earth, in combination with the heavy rains twice a year, the walls looked clean and white and the interiors were all bright and airy. Sister Ita's community numbered eight nuns, all of whom were medically trained in some form. This was apart from Sister Mairead, who doubled as the hospital secretary and housekeeper at the convent. She had arrived out a couple of months before us for her first stint in Africa and was also still wet behind the ears. Sister Ita Barry had worked in Uganda for the best part of twenty-five years and had had a wealth of experience running small bush clinics in Kenya before coming to Kitovu to organise her first big project. She spoke Luganda – the language of the Baganda people – fluently, even to being able to haggle aggressively and tell jokes with panache. She was a trained nurse and midwife. When the sister pharmacist was ill she stepped in and made up prescriptions, and when the Ugandan laboratory technician went off to get married, she busied herself with the stains and the microscope and did all the parasitology for a week. The more I grew to know her the more desperate I became to find one area of the hospital where she could not pick up the reins and deputise efficiently.

The doctor's bungalow was about 800 metres from the hospital compound and set within its own small garden. We were happy to continue with Fulgensio, the same houseboy who had worked for our predecessors, as Sister Ita indicated that his English was good and that he had a gentle way with children. Such recommendations were amply proved right over the next two years, and this thin twenty-year-old whose parents could only afford to put him through seven years of primary schooling, taught us a great deal about the Baganda people and instructed us in his language (Luganda), as well as cooking and cleaning. Jonathan, who was then just past his first birthday, had a very close relationship with Fulgensio, who called him 'Jolson' and seemed to earmark him for a career in music. Claire, being two and a half, found that she could give Fulgensio the slip at some stage during the morning when he was distracted, and she would make her way down to the convent, usually in time for the mid-morning coffee break in the sisters' dining room.

The hospital generator provided electricity for two hours in the morning and four hours each evening, although early in our tour of duty we were connected to the mains supply, which felt really luxurious. Water was pumped up the hill from a covered well in the valley each morning and evening, filling the small storage tank in our gable end, but it retained the colour of the soil so red, shared baths became the norm. I never did understand how Fulgensio managed to get the washing so clean with this water – and without a trace of the red earth that tainted everything else.

The day after our arrival at Entebbe I started work at the hospital, and this initially involved a ward round on each of the four wards to get to know the patients, followed by a session with Mr Ddungu, the hospital secretary. This grey-haired, sombre man had taken early retirement from the civil service in Kampala to be near his family home in Masaka and now worked for the Sisters, mainly in the areas of staff recruitment, discipline and running the finances of staff wages and 'billing' patients. All patients attending mission hospitals throughout East Africa at that time had to make some payment for their treatment, and although this amount was small in European terms, it was appreciable for the average Ugandan family. As a result they often had to save for any elective surgery, whilst an emergency admission to hospital meant either borrowing money to pay the hospital bill or negotiating a loan from Mr Ddungu. Coming from a National Health Service where no money changed hands, I found this a difficult concept, especially in a poor third world country.

The alternative for the patients was a government hospital where everything was free on the surface. In reality there was overcrowding on all the wards; the staff were poorly paid and not well motivated so often resorted to unofficial bribes before providing such essentials as a bed pan, which were usually in very short supply anyway. Many local people I spoke with indicated that the unofficial costs for a patient in a government hospital were similar to the basic bill at a mission hospital but without the quality of care.

I returned home at lunchtime to find Fulgensio in reasonable control of the kitchen and lunch. His progress had been slowed by the discovery of a small black snake coiled up in the cupboard under the kitchen sink. With the house empty for a few weeks the various hazards of life in East Africa had come onto the scene, and I was anxious to know the identity of this snake and, if poisonous, whether we carried the appropriate antisera in the hospital dispensary.

'What sort of snake is this, Fulgensio?'

'Ah! It is a very dangerous snake, Doctor, so I killed him very quickly.'

'Yes, thank you for killing it so quickly, but what is its name in Luganda?'

'It is called *enyoka* in Luganda, Doctor, it is very dangerous.'

Defeated by my lack of Luganda I took the reptile in question down to the hospital later that afternoon and decided to pursue the identification exercise with the redoubtable hospital secretary.

'Good afternoon, Mr Ddungu. My houseboy killed this in my house this morning and I wonder if you know what it is by any chance?'

'Aiiiee, Doctor, that is a snake!'

'Yes, but what sort of snake is it?'

'A very dangerous snake, Doctor.'

We were not making much progress in rationalising the use of the antisera so I played the Luganda card.

'What is *enyoka* then, Mr Ddungu?' I asked, thinking that Fulgensio had more of a feel for the wildlife than this city dweller.

'Ah that is Luganda for a snake, Doctor.'

We had come full circle, but Mr Ddungu was interrupted by Sister Ita passing by his door who looked in and casually said, 'At least it's not a black mamba!' for which I was greatly relieved. She then went on to add: 'Talking of black and snakes, you ought to get hold of a black stone for your emergency bag.'

Sister Ita then explained that in the early days of the White Fathers' efforts to establish missions throughout East and Central Africa, a Belgian priest was working on the borders of the Congo and Uganda when he was shown a black stone by the local people that was supposed to counteract the effect of poisonous snake venom. A cut was made over the snake bite and the stone was pressed to the skin. Within a few minutes the stone adhered to the incised area with blood and serum oozing out of the wound. It remained adherent until the mineral had removed the venom, whereupon the stone would drop off. Great care was needed at this stage to ensure that the stone was not damaged by falling onto a hard surface. The stone was then placed in milk for twenty-four hours before being dried and it was then ready for use again. I searched Siter Ita's face for the hint of a wink or a smile, as this all sounded a bit far-fetched, but her expression remained serious and she affirmed that most of the priests carried a black stone with them on their travels. The doctors working at Kitovu Hospital had always placed their trust in the small bottles of antisera in the fridge but she would be interested to see the effect of the two agents working together.

The White Fathers is a missionary society of priests and brothers founded in North Africa in 1868 by Charles Lavigerie, the then Archbishop of Algiers. Ten years later its members started the first Catholic missions in Kenya and gradually extended out from there. The White Fathers followed a lifestyle very close to the people amongst whom they were working and brought with them the traditional clothing of North Africa, the tunic and burnoose (a hooded cape), both white. When I first arrived in Uganda only the older priests continued to wear this habit on an everyday basis; its effect was always both dramatic and comforting at the same time.

An invitation to a seminary run by the White Fathers some twenty miles into the bush might present an opportunity to acquire a black stone. At this institution an enterprising young priest had organised the importation of what he euphemistically called exotic cattle. These Fresian/Holstein cows had been donated from farms in northern Europe and at this altitude were reckoned to be unlikely to contract the feared rinderpest that was endemic in Kenya. Even so they had to be tethered under shade throughout the day and their grass cut for them by an army of little boys. The student priests were taught husbandry as part of their training to be self-reliant when living in the more isolated parts of the country. Looked after in this pampered way these cattle would give twenty to forty times the milk yield of the average Ugandan cow.

As we arrived with the children that afternoon to look around the farm, I was informed that one of their prize heifers had a retained placenta after a difficult delivery of a healthy calf and did I know anything about removing this placenta. The nearest vet was in Kampala, some two hours' drive away, so even if he were immediately available there would still be a long wait. Realising that I might have to earn my black stone, I volunteered.

I now know that whereas a human placenta is made up of many cotyledons or lobes that are usually coalesced in the one mass, the placenta of the cow is also made up of similar cotyledons but they are all separate and discrete and thus have to be removed from the uterus one by one. This is an exhausting process made doubly difficult by the need to perform this task buried up to the armpit in the cow's uterus. For days afterwards the bovine aroma would reach me from my right elbow or upper arm and only many years later did I learn that vets come equipped with long gloves which extend to the armpit for these procedures and not the simple surgical gloves which I had used. Still, the gratitude of the White Fathers extended to providing me with a black stone which I kept in my emergency bag for the following six years in East Africa and had occasion to use on four or five occasions, but always in conjunction with antiserum.

A few weeks after acquiring this black, shiny slate-like material, an Asian lady was brought to the hospital in the early evening in a state of collapse. She had been walking in her garden at dusk in open-toed sandals and had obviously disturbed or trodden on a snake which had bitten her on her second toe. The pain was intense and the family realised what had happened, but even so the journey to the hospital took slightly more than ten minutes. No one thought to put a tourniquet around the toe, which would probably have saved her life, and so by the time we saw her she was moribund. The black mamba has a reputation for being one of the world's most poisonous snakes and was certainly fairly common in this part of Uganda. This poor lady died within a few minutes of arriving at Kitovu, and neither antisera nor the black stone could be used with any advantage. Our small hospital recorded an average of four deaths each year from snake bite; taken in conjunction with the much larger government hospital in the town, plus all the unreported snake bites out in the villages, the total number of fatalities in the district must have been considerable.

The sisters at Kitovu maintained a strong sense of community and we were privileged to be included not only in the celebrations at the convent for the high days and holy days but also in 'elevenses' each morning. Work at Kitovu would start on the wards, clinics and theatre at eight o'clock before this informal gathering for coffee after the first 'shift' gave a chance for everybody to catch up with what was happening in other departments. At this daily gathering the sisters would often reminisce about the early days of their work in Uganda. The generation before them occupied much attention at times and it was during one of these sessions that they quoted one of the memories of an elderly White Sister who, along with two other nuns, walked up to Uganda from the Kenyan coast with one bicycle shared between them. They arrived at their mission where the White Fathers were already well installed, but in those days there were very few doctors so this young White Sister, being a trained nurse, had to take over all the medical responsibilities. Whenever one of the White Fathers needed an injection (usually chloroquine for their malaria attacks) then she had to administer the treatment. But Church law forbad a nun to see the bare backside of an ordained priest, so the suffering father would back up to the green curtain of the cubicle and the young sister would feel the target area through the material before dabbing a spot of spirit on the cloth and then give the injection. From time to time Sister Roberta, who was the pharmacist, would receive a parcel of drugs collected and donated by general practitioners in her native Tyneside. These antibiotics or analgesics would then be announced as priority prescribing status, in order to ensure that everybody was aware of their immediate availability and that these valued gifts were used within the period of their shelf life.

Claire quickly realised that life was a bit more interesting beyond the garden gate. With her mother out running mobile child health clinics in the villages and her father working at the hospital, it was quite easy to dodge Fulgensio and make her way down to the hospital wearing her large straw hat and clutching a favourite doll under one arm. Approaching the hospital from our bungalow the first building encountered was the operating theatre, and so it was that we were just finishing one of our lists in those early weeks when the door opened ajar and a little head topped by a straw hat peeked around. Instead of shouting to maintain the privacy of the operating theatre Sister Ita asked one of the theatre nurses to give Claire a face mask to wear and once we had finished the operation she invited Claire to join us in the convent for coffee and home-made biscuits. After that Claire missed out on the hospital bit and went straight to the sisters' dining room, arriving on time each day, without a watch or even being able to tell the time.

She struck up a good friendship with Sister Mairead, who was in charge of administration and running the convent. Mairead had arrived out in East Africa just a few weeks before us and joined us on a steep learning curve, both with the language and the customs. A great deal of food was purchased fresh at the back door, and whilst this was mainly fruit and vegetables from the local farmers, occasionally it ran to chickens or goats. Coffee was interrupted one morning in those early weeks with Mairead proudly showing a couple of hens which she had just bought from two small boys at the back door. The hens' legs were bound with the traditional banana fibre and the birds themselves looked decidedly plump and well cared for; quite a contrast from the usual Ugandan fowl, which took free range to an extreme. Sister Ita glanced up at the purchase.

'I think if you check the coop around the side of the house, Sister, you will see that you have just bought two of your own hens.'

After this Claire was detailed to make sure that she knew each one of Mairead's hens to avoid any repetition of these events. Generally I was very impressed by the sisters' business sense, especially the sharper aspects of Sister Ita's grasp of taxation. When we had agreed the terms of my contract in London during the early part of the summer I realised that the sisters could not afford an attractive salary but they made up for some of the shortfall by providing free accommodation. Once I had decided on a car, which was a new Toyota estate, I worked out that I could afford the vehicle only if I had a loan from the convent, so that the cost of the car would be deducted from my monthly salary over the two-year contract. Sister Ita soon had all the figures in front of her and then calculated that she could not only make this loan interest-free but also deduct it from my salary before tax was calculated. I therefore signed for a new monthly salary figure long before I received my first pay cheque, and was then in receipt of free accommodation and transport before being assessed for income tax.

Sister Ita's financial skills also extended to the relatives of patients who were temporarily short of funds when it came to settling their hospital account. As a result of the length of time she had spent in this area, plus her knowledge of the local people and their customs, she would come up with a plan to defer payment until they had harvested and sold their coffee crop or make arrangements for small monthly payments, but all free from interest or penalty. The patients and their relatives held Ita in high regard and her implied trust in them and their family was reciprocated in the patients' attitude to the hospital. If we recommended surgery as a treatment for their condition then they would usually agree without question. The only proviso was that anything removed from their patient would be available for inspection by the family with some sort of explanation.

Usually this presented no great problem. The fibroids of the uterus grow to a large size in the African woman and ovarian cysts and thyroid goitres are also often sizeable by the time the patient brings the condition to medical attention. A small piece could be removed and submitted to the pathology department at the University Hospital in Kampala whilst still leaving a large part to impress the relatives. So it was that on my operating days of Tuesday and Thursday little groups of relatives would gather in the early morning on the small grassed area just outside the door of the operating theatre. I would be walking down to the hospital about the same time and after the first few weeks I noticed that a group of vultures had gathered on the roof of the theatre building. These ugly big birds graced us with their presence only on operating days and I was lost for a rational explanation. Lost, that is, until I came out of theatre during an operating list to attend to a patient who had collapsed on the ward nearby. I then saw the last lot of relatives wandering off, having seen and inspected the large fibroid uterus which had been handed to them by Damiano. But instead of pushing the large specimen back through the door into theatre they left it in the stainless steel dish on the grass and this is where the vultures came in. Damiano, who came from the west of Uganda, just assumed that these Baganda people took the specimens home with them. Once we tightened up the disposal procedure the vultures left us alone, and I was enormously relieved not to have to work with this image of vultures on the operating theatre roof.

The only time I can ever remember seeing Sister Ita defeated was when one young woman refused to have the skin sutures removed after surgery for an ectopic pregnancy, being fearful that once these stitches were taken out then the air would rush in and she would swell up. No amount of persuasive reasoning changed the young patient's mind and in the end I suggested that no harm would come of letting her go back to her village; the stitches would work loose over a few months and be extruded.

Four months after starting with the sisters at Kitovu I received a distressing phone call from my mother in England informing me that my father had lost his battle against lung cancer and had died. Just before we left England my wife and I had visited him, with our two small children, as he lay in a hospital bed at the Brompton Hospital awaiting lung surgery for a tumour. He did not wish us to delay our departure nor in any way postpone our plans on his account, but made me promise to return and be with my mother for a short while in the event of his death. After undergoing surgery he was informed that it had not been technically possible to fully clear all of the tumour, and being a physician himself he had declined radiotherapy. I made arrangements to return to England as soon as possible, leaving my own small family at Kitovu. Again Sister Ita was indispensable in helping me to find a cheap flight at short notice, and helping me to pay for it with an unsecured loan. I had time to pack a few clothes in a suitcase as I prepared to leave Kitovu at 5.30 the following morning to drive to Entebbe to catch the flight. Joseph, the hospital driver, was in Kampala visiting family and he would be able to bring my car back from the airport.

I kissed my wife and the children goodbye, the latter as they slept tucked up with dolls and teddy bears, and drove off into the darkness. By the time I reached the wide marsh area there was just a hint of dawn in the sky ahead of me and travelling at a good speed on the tarmac road, lined by the tall papyrus grass on either side, I was struck by the emptiness of the road at this time of the day. Travelling a tad too fast I was fortunate to see a rounded grey shape ahead of me and was able to stop just in time. A large hippopotamus, which formed this obstacle to my progress, just trundled a few more yards along the metalled road before finding its usual access point to the deep water of the marsh. These animals come out of the water at night to graze and, being a very close match to the grey colour of the tarmac, constitute a hazard just before dawn and immediately after dusk. I had recovered my composure after a few miles and, anxious to check in early at the airport, had again increased my speed. This time there was enough light to see the obstacle of a Ugandan police roadblock manned by four men with semi-automatic guns. Such roadblocks were a common feature of life around the Baganda region at that time, as Milton Obote constantly feared the effective opposition in this part of the country, the heartland of the Baganda people. Any car approaching a roadblock at speed always raises the tension and again I came to a halt only feet from the obstacle and the guns were pointed at me. I explained to the senior officer who I was, where I had come from and why I was hurrying to catch a plane for England. In impeccable English he lectured me:

'I am so sorry about your father, but you are now the head of the family. You must act responsibly and not make this a double funeral.' As he waved me on my way he added: 'Please give my greetings to your mother.'

Twelve hours later I was back in London on a cold damp January night.

## *Chapter Two*

I spent three weeks in England after my father's death, and following such a family bereavement there can never be a 'good' time to leave a mother and return to one's own young family and a job several thousand miles away. My sister was still working from the family home and my mother planned to have her own mother to come and live with them after a while so there would be support and company. I managed to find a cheap charter flight back to Entebbe, but in those days there were strict regulations about passengers on a charter belonging to the organisation for which such a cheap fare had been made available. So I became a member of an association studying tropical botany and just about managed to follow any conversation drifting in my direction from my fellow passengers.

Joseph, the hospital driver, met my flight at Entebbe and we drove straight back to Kitovu where I was given a great welcome by my family and the sisters.

Fulgensio greeted me profusely with the traditional Luganda greeting to which I could now respond:

'You are visible.'

'I am visible.'

'The lake is calm.'

'Yes. The lake is calm. Hmmm.'

'How are you?'

'I am well. Hmmmm' (even though I was exhausted and emotionally drained).

'How are those at home?'

'They are well' (even though my mother was very alone and tearful).

'How are they at your home? Hmmmm.'

'They are well. Hmmmm.'

Only after this routine did he enquire, 'How are they at home, Doctor, and how is your mother now?'

Throughout my time in East Africa I was always impressed by the way the people were able to place themselves right inside your life and speak with such sensitivity. If you accidentally hit your head on a doorpost they would apologise: 'Oh! I am so sorry' – even though the door had nothing to do with them. Yet, if they accidentally broke a cup in your kitchen they would declare: 'When I came I found it broken' – a mixture of not attempting to hide the breakage but also not accepting responsibility.

After my enforced absence from work for the best part of one month I made strong efforts to catch up with the backlog of operations that had built up during my time in England and also discussed with the sisters the need to expand the amount of private work at Kitovu. The money generated by increasing the volume of the work and raising the charges for private maternity care could then be directed to the fast expanding child welfare and malnutrition programme.

The Asian community became well established in all three East African countries during the building of the railways in the early part of the nineteenth century when the British brought artisans over from India to work on construction, maintenance and the running of the network. Inevitably most of the workers settled and brought their families over to join them. Rapidly they developed skills away from the railway industry, with most showing a penchant for trading, although the majority of Sikhs remained loyal to their roots and often set up engineering firms, carpentry workshops and, later, vehicle maintenance. At that time in Uganda most of the larger shops and private businesses were owned and run by Asians, who were generally courteous and helpful, although often the English was a little quirky. One young mother attending the antenatal clinic for her first visit was questioned:

'Is this your first pregnancy?'

'Oh no! I have two children; one is five and the other is half past two.'

Communication has always been very important in clinical medicine. The patient always feels more confident and reassured if their doctor understands and speaks their own language. For my first few months I had to work through a nurse translator and this became very frustrating at times.

'Has the patient had this pain before?'

This question would then be posed by the nurse, and the patient would reply at length. Then a further comment from the nurse and more explanation from the patient. At the end of what seemed like a great contribution to the history of the illness, the nurse would turn to me and say:

'No.'

'But what was all that conversation about then?'

'Oh nothing. This patient does not understand very well.'

This provided a great stimulus to learn the more important clinical phrases in Luganda and so avoid the intermediary.

In the nearby town of Masaka most of the Asian businessmen drove the eighty miles to one of the three private hospitals in Kampala if they or one of their family fell ill. Now that Kitovu Hospital had a well-equipped operating theatre and safe anaesthesia, along with several private rooms, we embarked on an aggressive marketing campaign whenever we went shopping in the town. But in Africa word of mouth can be the most important vehicle and our reputation was enhanced when the wife of a successful Asian businessman in Kampala was visiting her family in Masaka one weekend and developed a serious complication in late pregnancy. She had complained of abdominal pain followed by vaginal bleeding and then became increasingly weak. Her parents brought their young daughter to Kitovu and it was soon obvious that she had an unusual problem of the placenta separating before she had even started in labour. I explained the situation to them; the baby's heartbeat was becoming fainter as its blood supply was being threatened. The only hope for both the baby and the mother was to carry out an emergency Caesarean section. There was certainly no time to drive her to Kampala and to the hospital where she had been booked to have her baby. The operation and anaesthetic went smoothly and we had a healthy baby boy delivered within thirty minutes of making the decision to operate. The mother needed a blood transfusion to make up for the bleeding and the huge blood clot behind the placenta, but by the time her husband arrived from Kampala two hours later she was sitting up in bed and expressing her joy and relief.

Sultan and his young wife and baby were Ismaili Muslims, followers of the Aga Khan, and this community formed the largest group of the Asian people living in Masaka at that time. They showed embarrassing gratitude both to the sisters and to me after the successful outcome of the pregnancy and insisted that our family stay with them in Kampala whenever we chose to visit the capital. With a large house and garden, plus a swimming pool, in a quiet suburb, we spent several weekends with them and watched little Moezin grow up. Then, when the baby was just one year old they moved to Vancouver in Canada; political tension was rife in Uganda and they anticipated the changes that made many of their kith and kin leave in a great hurry one year later. During the weeks that followed this emergency Caesarean we had many Asian patients transfer their antenatal care from Kampala to Kitovu and soon I was able to persuade the sisters to change the scale of our private fees to match those of the private hospitals in Kampala – a fivefold increase.

Mr Ddungu was sceptical: 'This is too much money, Doctor, these people do not have that sort of money.'

But Sultan had told me exactly how much money a local merchant would make from his successful *dhuka* (shop) and after a few months we had no problem in collecting payment and the private wing was always full.

Sometimes the expectations were flattering. One lady came all the way from Mbale (100 miles north of Kampala) for an outpatient consultation as she had heard that a gynaecologist was working at Kitovu who could help infertile women. This lady was nearing sixty and had not had a period for ten years. I had to explain to her that although I was performing surgery on blocked tubes in younger women with infertility, the challenge that she posed was just too great.

Unfortunately there was a great local demand for removal of the tonsils amongst Asian young adults and children, whilst the Africans seldom seemed to suffer from chronic tonsillitis. The sisters took several bookings for this operation and this threw me into a quandary. Whilst training at King's I had had to have my wisdom teeth extracted whilst I was attached to the Ear, Nose and Throat Department and so missed out on tonsillar surgery. After three evenings engrossed in a textbook of operative surgery I felt that I knew my way through the procedure fairly well, even though we lacked the one essential instrument for the operation: the tonsil snare. Many of the older books refer to the operation being done by the local GP with the child sitting upright on the edge of the kitchen table and the assistant administering anaesthesia in the form of a rag and a bottle of chloroform. For me to perform the operation safely I would have to anaesthetise the patient with a tube going up the nose and then down the back of the throat and into the trachea. The back of the throat would then have to be packed with gauze to prevent blood running down alongside the tube. Only after this could the tonsils be dissected out with long instruments. Fortunately, with these safeguards in place, every tonsil operation at Kitovu went smoothly and successfully. The sisters were quick to give credit elsewhere: 'Thank God, that all went very well.'

This was a battle I could not win. Operations on patients with large malignant tumours were frequently unsuccessful and in that case they would say, 'Never mind, Doctor, you tried your best.'

For all the sisters' devotion to their calling I never once recall any attempts at conversion. If the Asian community was diverse then so were the local African Christians, with Anglicans, Seventh Day Adventists, Methodists and Baptists all represented in a local Roman Catholic majority.

The only time I can recall any sort of 'interference' was when Sister Monica, who was in charge of the surgical ward, indicated that a man of about forty was a bit reluctant to agree to surgery on his bowel problem because he was anxious about his wife. It emerged that he had been unable to pay the 'bride price' to his wife's father and so they had lived together with the intention of paying the requisite number of cows and goats after a few years and then going ahead with the wedding ceremony. Children came along and this economic drain meant that he had never actually been properly married to his wife. The thought of undergoing surgery with its risks of leaving her a widow, but without the respect of marriage, caused a problem. When I came onto the ward and asked about his religious denomination the staff nurse told me in her blunt way:

'He is a pagan, Doctor.'

This could mean that he was either not a Roman Catholic like her or he had just not got around to finding religion either. Within a few minutes Sister Monica had found the hospital chaplain (Father Dennis) and had press-ganged the staff nurse and myself to act as witnesses and produced her ring (nuns wear a ring on their fourth finger after their final vows) for the ceremony. The patient then went into theatre for surgery still wearing Sister Monica's ring and only returned it to her ten days later just before he returned home with his new wife to their five children and to face the music with his elderly father-in-law.

It was standard practice in most hospitals in Uganda for several members of the patient's family to accompany them to the hospital. Not only were decisions on surgery or treatment made by the family in consultation with the patient, but throughout the stay in hospital the family members bought and cooked food for 'their' patient. In the government hospitals this was often essential as the money available for patients' food was low in priority alongside the costs of drugs and treatment. The mission and private hospitals reduced the inpatient charges if the patients were fed by their family. A great medical advantage of a number of relatives was the ready availability of blood donors. Most patients admitted to hospital in Uganda at that time were anaemic to some degree, either from chronic malaria, hookworm or nutritional deficiencies, and a clutch of relatives willing to donate blood was always a great advantage.

Two conditions that were frequently encountered – ruptured uterus in labour and ectopic pregnancy – often resulted in severe blood loss, usually in excess of any supply available from even the best intentioned family. We managed to run a small blood bank which depended on blood donated by relatives for major elective surgery not actually being needed at the operation. Ectopic pregnancy occurs at about six to eight weeks of pregnancy when the developing sac has become stuck in the tube and has not passed into the main body of the uterus. A normal pregnancy demands a rich blood supply as it develops but the thin walls of the tube – not designed to hold a pregnancy – usually rupture at an early stage. This results in internal bleeding causing severe pain and shock and by the time the young woman has been brought in from her village she is often very weak. The emergency operation to remove the pregnancy sac and stop the bleeding often demands a replacement of six or seven pints of blood. As the blood from this condition leaks into the sterile peritoneal cavity there is a chance that it can be collected and transfused back again. I had only seen this method used once at King's College Hospital during my training but the sisters at Kitovu were well set up for such a procedure. A large stainless steel ladle, funnel and collecting jar (all sterile) were placed alongside the usual instruments and the blood was ladled out of the peritoneal cavity and poured into the collecting jar, via the funnel with a fine cotton gauze to strain out any small clots. A small quantity of sodium citrate in the jar ensured that the blood did not clot before it could be transfused back into the patient. With this system we were often able to auto-transfuse five or six pints of blood back, thus needing only one or two pints from the family to start off the resuscitation process.

The unpleasant experience and considerable risk of an ectopic pregnancy, which is still all too common in East Africa, can only be reduced by early awareness of the condition and this, in turn, is dependent upon the woman being aware that she could be pregnant. As the first signs of an ectopic become apparent some two weeks after the first period has been 'missed' the timescale is very important. Soon after I arrived in Uganda and was able to speak Luganda with some confidence, I found that eliciting the date of the last menstrual period was a little complicated. Many of the young women attending the clinic menstruated according to the four-weekly cycle of the moon. As the nights were clear and cloudless more often than not the standard reply to my question concerning the last period would be:

'When the moon was very small and over the lake,' or 'When the moon was nearly full and towards the west.'

My antenatal clinic quickly acquired a lunar calendar, in addition to my basic phrases in Luganda, to help me keep up with these answers.

The sisters provided accommodation close to the hospital in the form of a long brick building of individual rooms with a good roof and adjoining cooking facilities. This was the Bajanjabbe – the place of those who care for the sick – and during the day there was nearly always a wisp of smoke from the cooking area denoting that the kitchen was constantly busy. It was a running battle to keep some form of hygiene control in this area. The relatives could not be expected to be too meticulous and inevitably stray dogs came in from the surrounding villages to get quick pickings whilst the Kijanjabbe were with their patients. Soon these dogs became a real problem at night, roving through the open hospital walkways and frightening the nurses, so the sisters and I fell into a huddle to discuss how to cope with this unpleasant problem. These dogs had no owners, were covered with ticks and open sores from fights, and in addition presented a real risk of rabies. Shooting was not an option as no firearms could be held by the hospital, and as we wished to keep this as an internal matter we opted for poison. We bought a quantity of strychnine from the local chemist in the town, and then we all had to decide on a suitable bait for the dogs that ran no risk of accidental consumption by the relatives of the patients living in the Bajanjabbe. A suitable vehicle for the poison was a human placenta, but first we checked with Sister Catherine, the Baganda sister in charge of the maternity unit. She confirmed that none of the tribes in Uganda would ever consider keeping the placenta (the umbilical cord maybe, but not the placenta itself) and if they were to see one lying in the dust they would probably ignore it. With great care a generous spoonful of the powder was placed between the layers of the membranes of six placentae and then, last thing at night, these were left around the compound where the dogs commonly scavenged.

The next morning Kagwire, the sisters' odd job man, was quick to report to Sister Ita, 'Eh mnange, sister! There are six large dogs lying dead near the hospital. How can these big dogs have died so quickly during the night?'

Kagwire was a character straight from a novel by Thomas Hardy. He had a tremendous physique and usually had a spring in his step, with a hail and hearty disposition. But on Saturday evening, after receiving his week's wages, he would drink himself into a stupor and would hardly be seen on Sunday, which, by good fortune, was his day off.

'Well, Kagwire, would you please collect a wheelbarrow?' said Sister Ita, in a matter-of-fact way, 'then find someone to help you to take each of these dogs and dump them in the tip on the edge of the hill there.'

A week later we had another blitz that took out another five dogs, after which there was no further trouble from these intimidating creatures.

The student nurses on duty at night were now no longer afraid to walk the 400 yards to my bungalow with a request for me to come and attend an emergency in the hospital. We had no internal phones to the house so I was never actually aware that there was an emergency from the way that the message was brought. Being a light sleeper, I would wake up to hear the soft, slow footsteps on the gravel of the drive as the nurse approached the house. She would then come to the mosquito netting that covered the open louvres of the bedroom window and in a stage whisper would announce:

'They need you on Maternity, Doctor, there is a patient bleeding too much.'

Quite often I would scramble into a shirt and slacks, race down to the hospital and assess the patient before taking blood and setting up an intravenous drip. The sister would organise the relatives to donate blood whilst I would empty the uterus of the retained placenta under sedation. Not infrequently, as I started my walk home, I would pass the student nurse who had acted as the messenger, completing her return journey as she neared the hospital. Urgency, speed and hurry are essentially European approaches to situations, and given the climate in most of sub-Sahara Africa a slower approach has much in its favour.

With the clearance of the wild dogs we were aware of the need for some form of security, as our small bungalow was well away from the main hospital buildings and an easy target for petty thieves. The matter was finally decided for us when the battery of our car was stolen during the night from just outside our front door in the midst of a violent thunderstorm at the start of the rainy season. I went into the coffee break at the convent the following morning with a definite purpose and asked Sister Ita if she could order a replacement battery for me from the garage in the town and explained why the need had arisen.

'There won't be many cars starting first time outside the out-patients, so we might find a suspect quite soon trying to sell your battery, but in the meantime I will order you a new one. They say in Kampala that if your car wheels are stolen at night then it's best to get down to the market first thing and you could well buy them back quite cheaply.'

A visiting White Father, joining us for coffee, chuckled and related that the last time he was in Kampala a young Ugandan priest, who had just returned from his training and ordination in Rome, told him how he had suffered a puncture in one of the front tyres of his small Renault Roho. He had managed to find the jack and, kneeling down, had pumped up the front of the car to change the wheel. In this small vehicle the whole of the front of the car rose on the jack. As he was loosening the bolts a shabbily dressed local started to remove the other front wheel.

'What are you doing?' the young priest enquired of this intruder.

'Well, you're having that one, so I am going to take this one,' came the reply.

The local garage in the town provided me with a new battery and also took the opportunity to sell me a car alarm that operated on a trembler basis.

The first night that I set this new gadget we had another huge tropical storm and as the car was parked under a large avocado tree, every pear that fell off the tree in the strong wind and bounced onto the car caused the alarm to sound.

I was back in the convent for coffee the following morning.

'The car alarm seems to be a seasonal failure, I fear; are there any other suggestions that work in all weathers?'

Nobody seemed to have any ideas.

'I had thought about getting a dog just to alert us if any night time visitors come around again,' I ventured. 'Do you know of any puppies locally that might be suitable?'

I was secretly dreading the messing, chewing and yapping stages that this move would involve.

'Oh now, the midwifery tutor at Masaka Hospital told me of friends of hers with the British High Commission in Kampala who are due to return home soon,' said Sister Ita. 'They have a sausage dog and want to find it a good home. Get on the phone now and call Eve Osborne and she'll give you the details.'

Five minutes later I had spoken to the wife of the diplomat in Kampala and made an arrangement to collect the little dog the following Sunday afternoon. We had planned a weekend break in the nearest game park, and so we arranged to collect our guard dog on the return journey.

I thanked Sister Ita for this tip and expressed the hope that we would all be able to sleep more securely with a dog around, even though the dog was fairly elderly and would certainly not take to sleeping outside in a kennel at night.

'It all fits in very well, actually, as we are taking advantage of this offer in the *Uganda Argus* for local residents to stay at Paraa Lodge at cut-price rates for two nights. We can collect the hound on the way back. I guess you have all been to Murchison Park and seen the sights?'

'Do you know,' replied Sister Ita, 'I've been in the country for all these years but I've never had the opportunity to see a game park. We've been off to stay with sisters in Kenya and seen the animals in the wild, but never in a game park.'

'Well, what about it for this weekend – you and Sister Monica are due for a break and it is really very cheap,' I ventured. 'If you can put up with two small children then we can travel in the one estate car, and we will pay the park entrance fees.'

We left them to talk it over as a community and five minutes later I received a message to say that they would love to come with us.

In the overall scale of Africa, Uganda is a compact country, and our little party was able to leave Masaka in the morning and travel to Kampala and thence to Jinja to see the falls that are formed as the River Nile leaves Lake Victoria on the start of its long journey northwards. Soon after lunch we were in Murchison Park, which is divided into two parts by the Nile itself. We arrived at Paraa Lodge, set high on the bank above the river, and the family changed for a swim in the pool before the sun went down. The two sisters steadfastly refused to either bring or borrow swimming costumes but nevertheless, sitting on the edge of the pool, became very wet from the antics of Claire and Jonathan in the water. The next day we took the boat trip to the foot of the Murchison Falls where the River Nile bursts through a gap of eight metres and then falls forty metres into the game park, creating a constant cloud of spray. The river banks were studded with crocodiles basking on the mud, and the occasional elephant or antelope would warily break cover to come down to the water for a drink. It was our first experience of the wildlife of Uganda and it was wonderful to share those moments with two of the sisters who had worked for years in the country without ever venturing into the parks. Even now the game parks of East Africa are tourist attractions that are there primarily to generate hard currency. To this day the majority of the local schoolchildren in East Africa have never actually seen the natural history in the game parks of their own country.

Shortly after we drove through the park gates on our journey back we saw local fishermen selling their catch by the roadside.

'They will be Nile perch,' observed Sister Ita, 'and probably worth buying.'

Remembering the fleshy white fish that had been served the first night at the lodge for dinner, I pulled in and allowed her to lead the bartering. Not only was she pretty good in Swahili (for we were outside the area that spoke Luganda) but she was a great deal more experienced than I was in striking a bargain. The fish were huge – massive heads and scales the size of teaspoons. The one that Sister Ita eventually purchased would just fit across the back of the estate car with its tail curled up.

'That should give all of us a couple of meals!' she declared as she sat back in the car, but the expression on Claire's face indicated that she feared that she would be eating fish for weeks. We collected a smooth-haired tan dachshund from a house in Kampala that was in chaos with packing crates. We were informed that 'he answers to Raffles as he has a tendency to steal – especially food.'

Judging by his shape he had been singularly successful in this pursuit. With the doggy smell slightly balancing that of fish from the very back, the two hours to Masaka went quickly enough.

Raffles was a great surprise to Fulgensio who, in addition to calling the creature 'Rassles', took several weeks to get over the shape.

'But he has no legs, Doctor. How can he run and chase the thieves?'

'Once he has settled in and knows that this is his territory,' I explained, 'then I think he will behave like a dog, and the good thing is that he is small so he will not eat too much food.'

As anyone who has owned a dachshund knows all too well, this prediction came true within three days. Everyone passing the end of the drive triggered two or three barks and those venturing inside the garden area evoked a scurrying of short legs and incessant barking. The children walking back to their village from the local primary school shared Fulgensio's amusement but always maintained a healthy distance from the object of their ridicule. Raffles quickly became an affectionate member of the family and, with less opportunity to live up to his reputation, he slimmed down to a reasonable shape within a few months. As a child we had always had dogs but never this breed, however, Raffles became the first of many and even today in Somerset the house is ruled by two dachshunds – a brother and a sister.

Shortly after our weekend away, two of the sisters with a couple of nurses went off to a rural clinic that they ran every Thursday just off the main road between Masaka and Mbarara. The people in that area were predominantly the cattle-keeping Ankole but at that time their numbers were swelled by refugees coming across the border from Rwanda. Civil war had broken out and the tall Tutsi people were being hounded by the shorter, darker Hutu tribe. As the sisters were packing up after a long day, one of these refugee women gave birth by the roadside and was safely delivered of a baby boy. After a short while she and her elderly husband walked towards the main road to wait for a bus back to their temporary accommodation. As she sat down she must have disturbed a black mamba snake. According to witnesses she was bitten on the leg and within ten minutes was dead.

As there were no other relatives apart from the old man (being a refugee he had no family other than his young wife), the sisters offered to take the baby – named Karoli by his mother – back to the hospital until such time as he could arrange to look after him. Karoli was put in a side room off the children's ward, but after four weeks he had hardly gained any weight. Furthermore we were in the midst of a measles outbreak in the area and the children's ward was not a healthy place for such a young orphan. With a spare room in our house we decided that this little lad would be less at risk with us, and might also benefit from a more supervised feeding pattern. So it was that Karoli came to join us, and within a few days of continuing feeding problems we realised that he probably had an intolerance to cow's milk. A change to soya milk brought about better digestion and, with Fulgensio's help and devotion to a regular feeding regime, he soon started to gain weight.

In traditional African society it is usually the maternal grandmother who takes the responsibility for an orphan child resulting from death in childbirth. I remember the surprise at seeing one of these grandmothers breast-feeding a small baby in the maternity unit following the death of her daughter from a ruptured uterus as she was being brought to the hospital.

'As soon as I lost my daughter,' Sister Ita translated for me, 'I realised that I had to feed my grandson so I found a *muganga* (local doctor) and took some medicine.' She paused. 'After a few days the milk came through and I am happy.'

This lady was about fifty years old and indicated that her periods had just recently stopped as she entered the 'change', so thereafter we encouraged the younger grannies caring for their orphaned grandchildren to go to this local *muganga* for *dawa*.

The personal involvement in Karoli's nutritional problems led us to look carefully at the amount of instruction and advice given to mothers of young children, especially refugees and those Ugandan mothers living at some distance from their own tribal areas. An enthusiastic young doctor in Kampala – Michael Church – had set up the Mwanamagimu Clinic in the Government Hospital there, specifically to ensure that the children being weaned did not become malnourished when the mother became pregnant again. Traditionally, sexual relations were not resumed until the youngest child had been weaned – often at two years old – but changes in attitude meant that modern Ugandan women now conceived before the youngest child was even one year old. This little person was unable to stake his place at family mealtime and so often ended up with just the plantain staple (*matoke*) but little of the high protein groundnut sauce. The appetite is sated by the carbohydrate but there is no protein and this is the chain of events that sets in motion the disease of kwashiorkor. The face and limbs of the child swell as a result of this deficiency of protein and it typically occurs in tropical African countries where food is in good supply but the mother is unaware of the importance of nutritional values. With increasing numbers of children now being admitted to Kitovu Hospital with signs of kwashiorkor, we arranged for a group of our staff to visit Michael Church's clinic in Kampala to see if we could set up a similar facility, but on a smaller scale, in Masaka. We were all well aware of the chronic diseases in Uganda at that time, tuberculosis and leprosy, plus the long-term misery caused by polio, but the high death rate associated with kwashiorkor was very worrying. Uganda is a fertile country and this form of malnutrition could be eliminated by effective health education. At that time (the late 60s and early 70s) there was no sign of the scourge of Aids that has since swept through Uganda and other African countries. After some discussion with the sisters at the convent it was agreed that part of the children's ward would be given over to malnutrition rehabilitation. As these mothers were genuinely poor, or had no immediate family, they and their children would be treated free of charge. Gradually a small garden was established where the mothers could learn the ease and benefits of growing crops like groundnuts and local spinach. Many of these young mothers were first-generation shanty-town dwellers, having left their parents' rural homesteads in search of life close to the towns. Kitovu's allotment next to the children's ward was a valuable educational experience, and their child started back towards a balanced diet. Elizabeth's knowledge of Luganda and her skills as a teacher ensured that this clinic became well established and continued to function effectively until this entire part of Uganda became swamped by HIV Aids some fifteen years later.

Through this residential unit which was part of the children's ward we were able to learn some of the food taboos that were prevalent in the local community. The women in one district were convinced that the consumption of eggs led to female infertility. The local hens were very free range, often roaming for miles in search of food, and their produce, whilst small and inconsistent, was certainly nutritious, with wonderful orange yolks. However, with these eggs denied to all girls and women of child-bearing age this taboo seemed to have its roots in chauvinism. As a natural follow-on from dietary superstitions we were also informed about the medicinal benefits of certain plants and roots, and this was the start of a long-held interest in local medical practices. One young mother in the malnutrition clinic was expecting her third baby and showed us a preparation from the dried root of a plant rolled up in some mud.

'This is called *emumbwa*, Doctor, and when you feel that you are ready to have the baby you break off a small piece – enough to cover the nail of your thumb – and you take it with some water first thing in the morning facing the rising sun. You will then start contractions later that day.'

She assured me that many local women took this preparation. If that was the case, and if the preparation contained an active chemical ingredient, then the effects on the uterus could be very damaging, especially if the baby were too big for the pelvis. We therefore asked all mothers attending the antenatal clinic to come into hospital to take their *emumbwa*, so that we could monitor the effect of this preparation on the uterus and the progress of labour. From our experience over the following months, it became apparent that *emumbwa* was a powerful stimulant of uterine contractions, usually resulting in the onset of strong labour.

The local White Fathers told me of one of their missions in the west of Uganda, on the border with Zaire, where one of the priests had been analysing local medicines for several years, sending samples back to his native Germany for analysis. Michael Church from the Mwanamagimu Clinic in Kampala gave me the address of a friend of his just over the border in Zaire who would be worth a visit. So we set off for a few days' holiday to explore Fort Portal in the east of Uganda and the Ruwenzori mountain range that divides this part of East Africa from Zaire. Having driven past acres of tea estates as we approached Fort Portal we became aware that the combination of this crop and the coffee grown around Masaka must form a considerable part of Uganda's exports. The White Father mission was about thirty miles out of Fort Portal, in the foothills of this impressive snow-capped mountain range, which had so captured Henry Stanley's attention over 100 years ago. He resisted the pressure to label these the Mountains of the Moon and opted for the local name of Ruwenzori, which means 'rainmaker'. The Fathers had been collecting local medicinal herbs from parishioners for many years, and with true Teutonic thoroughness had catalogued the symptoms for which each preparation was meant to be effective. The results from the analytical chemist in Germany gave a good correlation for over 60% of the agents submitted, but as the Fathers pointed out to me, the real problem for the local medicine man lay in calculating the strength of the agent being supplied. If the plant is collected in the rainy season then the effective therapeutic agent will usually be more dilute. If collected in the dry season then the agent may be present in such quantities as to be poisonous.

Following our short stay with the White Fathers we went on to cross the border into Zaire, and this was our first experience of crossing a land border in Africa. Such border posts tend to be in sparsely populated areas, and at that time the majority of vehicles crossing were either lorries or buses full of people. I learnt from my Asian friends that whenever they crossed land borders some form of bribe was expected and offered for a 'trouble-free' passage. Whilst an expatriate vehicle obviously added a bit of interest and a change from the routine, there was never any hint or suggestion that money should be proffered. I sometimes wished that there was an agreed tariff to avoid the deliberations over the passports and the questioning that often followed.

'What is the purpose of your visit?'

'We are coming to visit a doctor friend and see his hospital.'

'Your face looks familiar. Have you visited Zaire before?'

'No. This is our first visit to Zaire.'

'But I have seen you before. Where have I seen you?'

'Perhaps you have visited Masaka in Uganda and you have seen me there.'

'No. I have not been to Masaka. But I have seen you before.'

Then the way out of this situation without risking further confrontation dawned upon me.

'Perhaps we all look alike to you. I assure you this is our first visit to Zaire.'

The border guard stamped our passports and let us continue on our way.

On that first visit we left the children in the car but the strategy we adopted for all future border crossings was to involve the children as much as possible in the routine. Without exception we found that the civil servants in East Africa were very tolerant of small children. Confident in this knowledge, we approached land borders by explaining to Claire and Jonathan that there would be a small office with lots of interesting rubber stamps on the desk. Now these rubber stamps, to the average immigration officer, are his prized possessions and indeed a sign of his power. One stamp will let you into the country and another will allow you to leave. Other stamps make it impossible for you to do either. Add to these the stamps that franked the date, the location of the post, diplomatic immunity and other variables and the threat that this collection might become an object of a children's play session made for a very quick processing of one's immigration formalities.

We were travelling to Zaire to meet up with a local doctor friend of Michael Church. Michael's parents had been missionaries in this part of Africa so his childhood years had been spent here. When he left for England to study medicine, a local Congolese childhood friend also left but on a scholarship to study medicine at Louvain, and he was now back and working in Zaire. We followed Michael's directions and eventually found a mud hut with a grass roof and introduced ourselves to a young man wearing a leopard skin. Tomas jovially explained that when he returned from his studies at a Belgian medical school he took over his father's traditional practice. He soon discovered that if he based himself at the local health centre and wore a white coat then he was only consulted by a minority of the local patients. By working from the family practice base in traditional costume he could reach most of the community and use herbal remedies. With great pride he slipped on a white coat and showed us round his new medical centre where he could treat that proportion of his patients who would benefit from what he called 'Western medicine' and could ensure that his immunisation and child health programme would reach a high proportion of the local population. He shared some of his hopes for the future with us and gave us a few tips on what to see locally.

'A few miles from here are some hot springs and thermal mud pools; perhaps we can develop this commercially like the spas that you have in Belgium and England. Do go and have a look, although you might find it a bit too hot for bathing. Oh! and be careful with the local pygmy tribe there. If you start taking photographs of them then they will demand money.'

We left to do the tourist bit.

# Chapter Three

After the best part of a year into the job I became increasingly aware of the vast network of missionary organisations across East and Central Africa that crossed the boundaries of religious orders, nationalities and even creeds. The Medical Missionaries of Mary are an Irish foundation and the majority of the sisters hailed from Ireland, but within our small community England, Scotland and the USA were also represented. The White Fathers and the White Sisters were founded in North Africa by a Frenchman, and throughout East and Central Africa the religious members were largely French, Belgian, Dutch and French Canadian. The Verona Fathers, an Italian foundation, were well established in the north of Uganda and the Italians were also very strong in the arid central area of Tanzania around Dodoma. All of these operated as a marvellous network, offering generous hospitality to any staff working with other missions in East and Central Africa.

The sisters seemed to entertain a fair number of visitors, with hospitals of their own in Kenya and Tanzania, staff from which often turned up for a few days' holiday in the pleasant climate that the proximity to Lake Victoria offered. The location of a seminary about half a mile from Kitovu which took students from schools all over Uganda to train for ordination into the priesthood meant that missionaries from the home parishes of these students often looked in for a few days. The boys from the north of Uganda found the readjustment particularly hard as they had to spend three years boarding in a college near Masaka. Not only did their appearance set them apart, with a much darker skin and finer facial features, but they found difficulties with the adjustment to a colder climate and a diet of plantains. One of these students consulted me on a regular basis during my evening surgeries at Kitovu with chronic abdominal pains. I soon realised that Joseph was very homesick for his family, who were Sudanese refugees living near Moroto in the north of Uganda. He was the only Sudanese student in the seminary and longed to hear and speak his own tribal language with someone.

'The pains in my tummy are because I have to eat these green bananas. At home I eat porridge from millet or sorghum and I think you should please give me a *cheti* (piece of paper) to say that I should have a special diet.'

I examined Joseph and found that he was tender in the lower part of his abdomen on the left side, well away from the stomach area, and I dismissed his symptoms as being psychosomatic, brought on by homesickness. A few weeks later he was brought over at about 11 p.m. in severe pain and with a history of being constipated for four days. He looked dehydrated and was obviously in severe pain, again in the lower part of his abdomen. We had to take him to the operating theatre immediately and whilst we ran in some fluid intravenously, we organised some blood and a general anaesthetic. Once inside his abdomen I found that the whole of his sigmoid colon (the terminal part of the colon that sits in the left side of the pelvis) had twisted on itself, shutting off the blood supply, and had become gangrenous. There was no chance of saving this part of the bowel and so this large purple loop had to be excised and I then joined up the healthy bowel on either side of this gangrenous portion. I inserted a drain into the area in case my stitches were stretched and leaked a little in the first few days and returned Joseph to the ward with plenty of sedation.

The next morning Joseph looked much more cheerful.

'I owe you an apology, Joseph, and I will give you that *cheti* for a special diet. I telephoned a colleague of mine in Kampala who is experienced in bowel problems in Africa. It appears that Nilotic people like yourself can have this sort of bowel problem if you go onto a heavy diet like *matoke* all the time.'

Joseph made a full and complete recovery whilst in Kitovu, but within days visitors arrived from Moroto, both family and some of the local Italian missionaries, who were very grateful to see him recovering. Our little family received a warm invitation to visit Moroto, with a recommendation to then travel further north and visit the remote Kidepo Game Park that runs close to the Sudanese border. With so few tourists visiting this area, the animals were really wild, perhaps more so because at that time there was a civil war in southern Sudan and many cross-border incursions took place into Uganda in search of game meat. As there was no lodge or accommodation in the Kidepo Park in those days we were pushed to consider a large tent that belonged to the seminary scout group. We accepted this offer gratefully and so we embarked on the first of our many 'camping safaris' throughout East Africa, the chief attraction of which was economic.

We packed the car during the late evening and were able to leave home after an early breakfast and headed for Kampala and Jinja before turning north towards Mbale. This town is in the foothills of the mountain range on the border with Kenya that is dominated by Mount Elgon, but during the journey onwards to our destination of Moroto the terrain quickly became flat, dry and dusty. It was late afternoon and the sun had already lost a lot of its ferocity when the engine of our large Toyota estate started to misfire. We were about twenty miles from Moroto and surrounded by semi-desert when the engine finally died. Just ahead of us was a tall Karamajong cattle herdsman. He was very tall and thin with a red blanket slung over one shoulder and on the other side he held a long spear. He left his herd of cattle and came towards our car, his loose-fitting home-made sandals kicking up puffs of dust. By that time I had the bonnet up and was looking at the small toolkit with some apprehension.

'Give it to me!' ordered the tall dark stranger by my side, holding out his hand. Hoping that another vehicle might soon come along and not wishing to take issue with the herdsman, I gave him the toolkit. He rested his spear against the car, and removed one or two tools from the kit. I went back to explain that this nice man was trying to help but could we all get out of the car and keep our eyes open for another vehicle of any sort. Returning to the bonnet I noticed that the plugs had been removed from the engine and were being cleaned with a mixture of spit and hard blowing, plus the occasional dab from the fringe of his blanket. The carburettor was then opened and cleaned before everything was carefully reassembled.

'Now start!' I was ordered.

Sure enough the starter fired the engine and we were returned to full power.

'Thank you very much,' I said, hoping that the surprise did not come through too strongly in my tone. 'Can I give you anything for your work and all your help?'

'No. It is nothing, but when you arrive in Moroto you must go to the mission and ask for the father who mends cars and he can look at it again.'

'We are staying there tonight,' I replied, 'so I will do as you say. But where did you learn about cars with all these cattle around you?'

'I was in the REME during the war,' my tall dark saviour replied, 'and once you have learned then you do not forget. But these are the cows of my father and my family and I must look after them now and not repair cars. *Kwahere* and *safari njema*.' (Goodbye and safe journey.)

He collected his spear, flung his red blanket back over his shoulder and strode off back to his herd whilst we put the car in gear and gratefully covered the remaining twenty miles to Moroto, receiving a warm welcome from the father in charge of the guest house. Leaving Elizabeth to settle Claire and Jonathan into our room and introduce them to the 'bowl and pitcher' method of washing with limited water availability, I followed the directions round to the rear of the mission where the vehicle service bay was located. I came across a charming elderly Italian man in dirty overalls who spoke very good English.

'We had some problems with our engine on our way here, Father. It started misfiring and then gave up altogether, so I would be grateful if you could check it for us. We were fortunate to find a local Karamajong herdsman who seemed to know his way around and got it going again.'

'Ah!' said the elderly cleric, 'I think I know who that would be. He is a trained mechanic and occasionally becomes a Good Samaritan. Let us have a look inside.'

I raised the bonnet and he brought round a machine to check the timing mechanism. Only as his hands went in to work on the engine did I notice a large ring on his right hand with an impressive amethyst stone set in its centre. I then realised that this was the Bishop of Karamoja District indulging in his special interest. This is the only occasion that I have had a vehicle serviced by a bishop, but a very good job he made of it and he gave much more security and comfort than the St Christopher medallions so favoured by the Catholic taxi drivers in Kampala.

The next day this humble car mechanic officiated at High Mass in his cathedral church, and we positioned ourselves at the back of the congregation, close to the main doors, just in case the children wanted to 'escape for a few minutes' during the sermon. I failed to appreciate that this place in the church was that usually occupied by the tenor and bass elements of the choir. These were impressively tall men with strong voices and wearing just the obligatory blanket over the right shoulder. Much of the music was their own tribal style adapted to the church liturgy and involved a fair amount of jumping up and down to emphasise the crescendos. Claire was mesmerised and tugged at my waist.

'Daddy! When the men sing I can see their willies!'

I tried to play this observation down, but Jonathan, whose vocabulary in this area was expanding quickly, took up the theme.

'What did Claire say about willies?'

We made a quick exit and had a few words of explanation about the way church services are conducted in different parts of the world before resuming our seats. When the Mass was over some of the choir invited us to come and visit their village nearby, as they seemed to be fascinated by two small European children with very blond hair. In common with other nomadic herdsmen like the Maasai and the Turkana, these people constructed their houses within a high ring of thorns in order to protect themselves and their livestock from scavenging animals and marauding rustlers from other tribes. We walked through the entrance in this tangled thorn fence and found ourselves in a well-ordered compound with roughly seven mud huts roofed with grass. Some of the elderly women who had not been at Mass were really fascinated by the children, and especially their hair, which they kept touching to feel the texture that was so obviously different from any hair that they had come across before. Both the children were irritated by this attention, but we explained that few people were given the privilege of seeing inside a Karamajong village and this was a sort of exchange. The elderly women seemed to approve of their small visitors and used a tribal way of showing their approval by spitting onto the tops of the heads of the children, before presenting them with gifts of beadwork bracelets and necklaces. Knowing the high incidence of pulmonary tuberculosis in these communities I was a little anxious not to gain too many visits to other villages. Jonathan filed this little custom away and used it on his fellow pupils on his return to school after the holiday, which fetched a remark from his teacher as we collected him, 'Could you please ask Jonathan not to go around spitting onto the heads of other children in the class?'

We made an early start the next day to travel into the Kidepo National Park and reach the campsite, which was a three-hour drive from Moroto. For the last hour of this journey we saw no sign of human life or domestic animals and so it was quite a relief to come across the park office and meet a very friendly ranger. He gave us directions to the campsite about two miles away and advised us to fill all our water containers here at the office, as the campsite was just a clearing in the bush.

'I think you should put out your campfire at night before you go to sleep, and you must keep a lookout for the snakes.'

We thanked him and then drove towards the campsite on a winding road fringed by tall grass. As we rounded one bend we suddenly came across two large bull elephants by the side of the road. We were as surprised as they were but somehow we were past them before we appreciated their presence. I slowed down in order to let the children have a better view, but these animals were obviously not used to tourists and made their intentions clear by charging us and trumpeting loudly. Thankfully, the Bishop's work on our engine stood us in good stead and we quickly left them behind.

We reached the campsite and unpacked the car to get at the scout group tent that had been loaned to us. As a general principle any tent should be assembled for the first time in the peace and quiet of one's own garden so that any shortcomings can be identified. In the middle of this remote game park we erected the tent frame, held it in place with guy ropes and tent pegs (that we could only just get into the very hard ground), but the fabric of the tent finished about six inches above ground level. With a warning about snakes, and assuming the presence of animals like hyenas at night, this gap could prove to be dangerous. Using our rudimentary tools we tried to sink the tent poles into the ground by about six inches and, after what seemed like a couple of hours, we had a reasonably secure accommodation assembled. A large campfire and a hot supper were then the priorities before the sudden African sunset at 6.30 p.m. Once the children were settled in their sleeping bags, I raked over the embers of the fire, but as our camping lamp was neither effective nor very reliable, I left a large amount of the fire glowing to give out a bit of light before climbing into the sleeping bag and falling asleep.

I was awakened in the early hours of the morning to hear Jonathan making noises of appreciation and satisfaction and thought that he was having some sort of dream. Putting on the torch I saw that he had hitched up the tent skirt and was looking underneath it out into the night. 'Ooh! Look. Ooh!'

Then I heard a roar and a snarl and I quickly pulled Jonathan back and looked out myself. The night had obviously turned very cold, as is the pattern in the semi-desert, and three maned lions were stretched out around our campfire embers. Soon we were all awake and talking in hushed whispers. Clearly the ranger had been correct in his advice (which we had taken in the context of fire risk to ourselves) and these animals had gravitated towards the heat during such a cold night. We lay awake for about an hour, occasionally peeping under the tent to look at these three lions as they struggled and pushed for the warmest place. Then all the heat must have gone from the embers for they shook themselves and stretched before they trundled off into the night. After that experience we made certain that all campfires were out and cold before we went to sleep during camping safaris.

We packed up the tent and camping gear the next morning and cleared the campsite before starting on our return journey to Masaka. After the three nights at Kidepo we had a good run back to Masaka and arrived in the early evening with no stopover in Moroto. We soon returned to the routine workload and I was humbled to realise that a patient had been quietly awaiting my return from this short holiday in order to see if I could repair a large rupture for her. As a result of several pregnancies in a short space of time this mother had developed a rupture through her umbilicus, and I agreed to try and repair it for her. As my knowledge of Luganda was limited, I was unable to explain to her the details of the operation, which would involve the removal of her umbilicus and a large ellipse of excess skin. The muscles through which the defect was protruding would then be repaired using a 'flap-over' technique and all that would show on the outside would be a linear scar across the mid line of the abdomen. The operation went well and I thought the patient would be delighted with the result, but when she came around from the anaesthetic and saw the scar she dissolved in floods of tears. It seems that the Baganda hold the umbilicus in special reverence and the tribal belief is that the 'tummy button' provides the link to the next world, whatever one's religious persuasion may be. I discussed this problem with Sister Ita and we suggested that the lady might come back in six weeks' time when we could fashion an artificial umbilicus into the scar at no cost to herself.

None of the operative surgery textbooks gave any hint on how such a procedure might be carried out, but employing the basis principles of surgery in reverse I was able to create a very convincing 'belly button' for this lady, who was delighted with the result. Such superstitions were by no means restricted to the African patients. On the odd occasion when a planned Caesarean operation was necessary on one of our Hindu private patients, the mother-to-be would have to go home first and discuss the proposed birth date with the astrologer. Only if she and her family were assured that this would be a lucky time to be born would she then agree to be admitted for the procedure. Superstition can often be associated with curses, and towards the end of that first year at Kitovu we admitted a young Sikh woman to the antenatal ward. She was ill and withdrawn and her husband explained the background.

'My wife was always the most beautiful girl in her family but last year she treated her cousin very badly and made her jealous. Her cousin cast a spell on her, saying that she would die in the seventh month of her seventh pregnancy.'

Looking at her case file I saw that although she was in her seventh month of this pregnancy she only had three children. I tried to reassure the anxious husband.

'Perhaps she did not tell you that she had three miscarriages before she succeeded in becoming pregnant with our first child.'

So strong was this young mother's conviction about the spell that had been cast upon her that she refused all food, turned her face to the wall and was dead within ten days. She spoke very little English, so the sisters and I could achieve little by way of communication. She took small amounts of food and fluid from her visiting relatives but to this day I cannot explain her death. The family declined a post-mortem examination and they took the body of the mother and her unborn child for cremation.

I had been growing increasingly aware of a painful big toe since the holiday in Karamoja, and on looking at the toenail I was aware that an infected ingrowing toenail was the cause of this pain. Antibiotic cream for a week gave no relief and I was faced with the decision of surgery, not just to remove the toenail but to cut away the root of the nail on each side to prevent a recurrence. It was possible to perform this procedure under local anaesthetic, but the nearest hospital with a surgeon was forty miles away and the operating theatre there was well below the standard of Kitovu. The risk of infection after the operation would therefore be considerable. I decided to operate on myself with the assistance of Damiano and Sister Ita, if they were agreeable. We fixed the procedure for a Saturday morning when the operating theatre was usually fairly quiet. I found that injecting the local anaesthetic was the most painful part of the whole procedure but eventually my big toe went numb. In a half-sitting position, and with Damiano handing the instruments and Sister Ita assisting, I tried to carry out the procedure but found that I was no longer supple enough to reach my big toe with ease and cut into the nail bed. Damiano then took over and he was able to remove a wedge of nail and part of the nail bed on each side of the big toenail. Sister then applied a dressing and I was driven the short distance back home to rest up for the weekend. A Dutch doctor and his family called in to see us on the Sunday afternoon on their way back home from a weekend in Kampala and I related my attempted do-it-yourself skills with a little pride.

'That's nothing,' he informed me. 'In a Dutch medical journal last month a doctor in the Congo wrote up how he had removed his own appendix. The heavy rains had cut off all the roads from his rural hospital. So he erected a large mirror above the operating table and with assistance from his theatre staff he removed his inflamed appendix under local anaesthetic over a two-hour procedure.'

I never made reference again to my little operation except to reassure any of my patients undergoing this procedure: 'I know this is a bit painful, as I have had it done myself.'

As I limped around the hospital the next day with a large dressing on my toe that gave the cartoon appearance of a severe case of gout, Sister Ita called me to see a case of tetanus that had just been brought in by a group of Ankole women who hailed from the neighbouring district of Mbarara. Occasionally a large herd of these Ankole cattle with their long horns and buffalo-humped backs would drift through the hospital compound in search of fresh grazing and the Ankole people, being predominantly semi-nomadic cattle herders, were particularly at risk for tetanus. This condition, commonly called lockjaw, is particularly distressing from a medical point of view. Even with today's sophisticated methods of treatment the mortality remains high, as the muscle spasms can be so severe that only the head and heels of the patient remain on the bed. The spores of tetanus can live in dry soil for many years but upon coming into contact with human blood and tissue through a small cut in the skin may be activated, with serious consequences. We had a comprehensive immunisation programme both in the hospital and the mobile clinics that immunised children against tetanus. Anyone presenting themselves with a fresh cut would be offered the anti-tetanus serum as the incubation period is over one week, but Sister Ita's greatest fear was infection of the newborn babies. The traditional birth attendant in the village would often use an old razor blade kept on top of the wooden front-door frame to cut the umbilical cord of the newly born child. With cattle around the hut, or drifting past the door at regular intervals, the risk of tetanus spores being on an old razor blade was obviously very high. We constantly emphasised the need for a clean new blade from a paper packet at every antenatal clinic, knowing that the majority of our expectant mothers would deliver their babies at home.

The week old baby brought in by her mother and a distressed group of relatives had been fitting for twenty-four hours and was already dehydrated. We set up an intravenous infusion into a scalp vein and used this to give Valium as well as to restore the fluid balance. At first the baby seemed to settle and the convulsions eased but later that evening the spasms returned and the outlook seemed hopeless. We explained to the sad little group that there really was no effective treatment for such a young baby. I woke a few hours later, in the early hours of the morning, to hear the unmistakable sound of wailing and howling that signified a death. With many of the patients' relatives staying close to the ward block in the Bajanjabbe they were readily on hand should any deterioration take place in the condition of their patient. The mourning process started as soon as death was confirmed and was spontaneous, loud and sincere. The intensity and duration of the mourning (it often went on for two or three hours) bore no relationship to the age of the patient or the length of the illness. Patients whose death in Western parlance would be described as a 'blessed release' were mourned with equal intensity as a child who died unexpectedly.

The Ankole people were taller than the Baganda, with slightly angular facial features, and moved around in strong family groups. Whenever Sister Ita was working in the morning outpatient clinic and we had a number of Ankole people around, she would always ensure that the generator was running for the X-ray machine. Most of the men were convinced of the healing powers of X-rays and demanded a chest X-ray for often the simplest cough. One other aspect of clinical care that had to be considered was that any medicine prescribed for either parent of the family was administered to the entire family, regardless of whether the others had similar symptoms. When the Ankole were 'in town' the large medicine bottles would be brought back to the clinic for a daily refill of cough or antacid medicine. One other endearing aspect was that the mothers expressed the ages of their children according to the charges in their care. Very young children would be called 'chicken watchers'; the five to nine year olds were the 'goat watchers' and the children who had roughly reached double figures in age were the 'cattle watchers'.

We were unexpectedly offered the chance of a weekend trip to Kabale District, the home area of Kagwire, the sisters' wonderful odd-job man. A family running a Church of England mission there had stopped over in Kitovu for a few days to spend time relaxing with their children down by the lake, and invited us for a weekend in the mountains of the far south-west of Uganda. The suggested plan of a day's trek into the Muhavura range of extinct volcanoes might afford the chance to see the shy mountain gorillas that live in the dense bamboo forest on these slopes.

As we reached Kabale town in the mid-afternoon of the Friday we were warned of the presence of local council road workers by the sign:

SLOW MEN
at work

We found that they were finishing off a speed hump to slow traffic down over the quarter-mile length of tarmac that graced the town centre. The only problem was that the speed hump which they had just finished looked very large indeed. They waved us over their masterpiece. I opened the door and explained that I thought the hump was too big.

'Not at all!' the foreman reassured me. 'Please drive on now, we want to finish work for the day.'

Predictably enough the car became stuck halfway and rocked to and fro with the drive wheels spinning. Fortunately the gang of workman was large and strong enough to push the car gently off the hump and we continued on our way to our friends' house, leaving the men to shave off the top of the hump.

'The men here are all as strong as Kagwire,' observed Claire.

We then had a three-hour journey over rough mountain roads, often in dense mist, to the little town of Kisoro where our friends lived and worked. The following day we spent an exhausting and wet foot safari tramping through dense bamboo and thick scrubby trees with a local guide on the steep slopes of the extinct volcanoes that tower above the town. We heard the gorillas just above us on the slopes and we saw one family group far away on the other side of the valley, but we were unable to get close to these magnificent creatures. By late afternoon we were pleased to see the family home again and the prospect of some hot water and a log fire for the evening.

The incidence of venereal disease in Uganda during the late sixties and early seventies was very high and this was long before the outbreak of HIV Aids which has since decimated the population in many countries of sub-Sahara Africa, often wiping out an entire generation. Gonorrhoea is a disease with far-reaching effects, resulting in infertility in many women and the risk of blockages in the urinary system in men. Working as a trainee surgeon in Plymouth many years ago I came across a group of patients, mainly veterans of the First World War or retired seamen, who had suffered the acute symptoms (a painful discharge from the penis) of acute gonorrhoea forty years earlier, and were now having to attend a hospital clinic to have urethral blockages (strictures) stretched. Curved metal 'sounds' were inserted to dilate the blocked part of the tube that carries the urine from the base of the bladder to the penis, and this procedure had to be carried out every six to eight weeks. When I arrived at Kitovu I found that we had a 'sounds clinic' for this problem, only with so many of the patients having to travel a considerable distance to reach the hospital, and the state of the roads in the rainy season, a regular attendance was often impossible.

I was fortunate to be able to attend a seminar in Kampala, run by a visiting specialist surgeon, that put forward a two-stage operation to remove the section of the urethra involved in the stricture and laying open the tissue. Then, at a later stage the urethra is refashioned. The surgeon demonstrated the success of his procedure by persuading six of his patients to stand behind a screen and then each to void into a galvanised bucket. The sound of the six buckets being hit rang around the lecture hall but this was nothing compared with the broad smiles on the faces of the patients as they came out from behind the screen, each clutching a bucket. After several months we were able to close our 'sounds clinic' at Kitovu, as all of those patients attending had undergone surgery. The most difficult part of coping with gonorrhoea was the health education needed to establish the link in the patient's mind between venereal disease at the age of twenty or so and a urinary stricture forty years later. More recently the health education workers have encountered similar difficulties in persuading communities to understand the method of transmission of the AIDS virus, with much more far-reaching implications.

With all the emphasis on nutrition and feeding children a balanced diet down at the Children's Unit in the hospital, and with little Karoli starting to thrive, our homestead was the object of several visits from mothers staying in the hospital. Some came to express gratitude for all the help and encouragement they had received in rehabilitating their child, not least educating the father in directing more of the family budget towards a balanced feeding regime for the children. Others came out of curiosity to see how we ran our house and garden. So it was that we felt we had to take our pets seriously and I was forced to construct proper cages and 'runs' for the rabbits and then learn a bit about poultry. We had been given one or two scrawny hens as presents and thought it would be worthwhile to rest their muscles a bit and fatten them up before considering them as a meal. Fulgensio was most dismissive of our efforts.

'These chickens are no good, Doctor, you must just cook them. Then you can buy small chickens from the fathers at the mission and these will grow into good chickens.'

He was right. A few hybrid day-old chicks would be on 'point of lay' after three months and would then produce a regular supply of eggs. Fulgensio despatched the broilers and then helped me to build a chicken coop with good protection from snakes and safari ants. We obtained a kerosene lamp and six little chicks, which we bought from the White Fathers Seminary of exotic cattle fame, crowded around it at night for warmth until their feathers had developed. Seeing our menagerie building up, some of the local lads came around with various livestock to sell to us. We accepted some duck eggs and were about to cook them when Fulgensio expressed some concern. A sheet of newspaper rolled into a tube and pressed to the egg, whilst the egg was held up towards the sun, showed that the yolk in these eggs had already started to develop.

'These eggs have been taken from a nest, Doctor, and they cannot be eaten.'

A recent gift of a broody hen was put to good use and a couple of weeks later two little ducklings hatched out and the broody hen took to her legs and paraded them around the garden. Raffles immediately showed an interest in these two fluffy yellow bundles but was chased off on more than one occasion by the combined forces of an aggressive hen and the screams of the children. The late afternoon was a perfect time of the day to sit in the garden for an hour or so; the sun had lost its heat by 4.30 p.m. and the mosquito population was rarely active until after dark. We had brought out a paddling pool in which the children were able to cool off when the weather had been particularly hot during the day. Without thinking, I splashed a few buckets of water into the pool one afternoon, but by the time Claire and Jonathan had finished their game and removed their clothes the two small ducklings were swimming around with great gusto, watched by their concerned adopted mother from the side of the pool. Real ducks in the 'bath' then became an obligatory routine each afternoon and Raffles backed right away from showing any further interest in these new additions.

Late one afternoon, when the paddling pool had been packed away for the day and the exhausted ducklings returned to their mother hen in the coop, two young Baganda boys appeared on the back doorstep asking if we were interested in two birds. I heard Fulgensio talking to them and went through to ask what was happening.

'These two boys have some small birds that they want to sell, but they are no good.'

I was not sure whether Fulgensio was referring to the shabby attire of the boys, whose parents could probably not afford the primary school uniform that was obligatory in order to take a place in the nation's free education system. I gave him the benefit of the doubt and assumed that he was talking about the even more shabby produce that they were selling. These ugly little birds had only just fledged and had long gawky legs and a 'punk' hairstyle set above two large eyes.

'What are they and where are they from?' I asked Fulgensio.

'They are wild birds, Doctor, and not good to eat.'

Clearly as a commercial transaction buying these two fledglings was not a good investment but, knowing that they would be left to die if we did not buy them, I offered the boys a shilling each for the birds.

'That is too much, Doctor,' opined my financial advisor at my side, but anxious for Fulgensio to return to his duties, I closed the deal and put the fledglings with the ducklings for the night.

As the weeks went by these birds became strikingly beautiful. Their legs became longer, their plumage took on some striking colours and the 'punk' style on top of the head gave way to a golden crown. In short, these were two crowned cranes, the national emblem of Uganda, and as such they appeared on bank notes, postage stamps and the national flag. Each night they took to roosting on top of the estate car, which annoyed Fulgensio whose work included a weekly cleaning of the car. As a result of the newcomers and the guano they produced this job had to be made more frequent. Primary school children used to stop on their way to school in the mornings to gaze at these lovely birds, having had few chances to see them at close range before. As they passed the end of the garden they would call out the Luganda name for the crowned crane, which is an imitation of the call the bird makes: 'Ngali, Ngali.'

The more accurate mimics were rewarded with a reply from one of the birds.

We fed them on hen food and some scraps from the kitchen. Any day when fish was on the menu brought them close to the back door looking for heads, skin or trimmings. At such times it was possible to view the delicate golden feathers that comprised the 'crown' on top of their heads and I was always struck by the thought that seldom can one shilling have been such a good investment. Eventually the inevitable happened and a flock of these cranes flying high overhead towards Lake Victoria called out on the wing. Our two charges looked up and without a great deal of internal turmoil left the roof of the car, where they were anticipating nightfall, and flew up to join the flock, never to return. Claire and Jonathan were a bit upset, viewing it as a reflection on the standard of hospitality that we had offered. The primary school children passing the end of the drive each morning were similarly devastated but Fulgensio was greatly relieved that this strange chapter was over.

## Chapter Four

The year 1971 brought significant changes to the people of Uganda and also upset the relationship with the two partner states of Kenya and Tanzania in the East African Community. President Milton Obote hailed from the relatively small Acholi tribe in northern Uganda. Having deposed the traditional king of the Buganda – the Kabaka – and dissolved the autonomous government of Buganda that had been agreed at Independence as a sop to the Kabaka, the President was never high in the popularity ratings amongst the Baganda people. Obote was very close to Odinga Odinga, a leading opposition MP in Kenya whose views were considered to be very left wing. There was even talk of Uganda supporting Odinga Odinga in a possible coup attempt against President Kenyatta. Britain had many interests in Kenya and also had troops stationed north of Nairobi to ensure a presence in the horn of Africa and the gateway to the Suez Canal.

Against this background the Commonwealth Prime Ministers' Conference, which had always traditionally been held in London, was to be hosted by the Singapore government. All three presidents of the East African states indicated their eagerness to attend this first meeting of Heads of Government outside the United

Kingdom and much was made of the coming event in the *Uganda Argus*. President Obote and his entourage flew out of Kampala on the Friday, and on the Saturday evening a young volunteer teacher from London who was working for a year in the local secondary school accepted an invitation to come and have a meal with us at Kitovu.

Halfway through the meal there was a gentle tap on the mosquito netting of the dining-room window. It was one of the nursing auxiliaries who acted as messengers from the sisters.

'There is a telephone call for the lady teacher from the school.'

Our guest left us and accompanied the messenger back to the convent, where the only 'outside line' was positioned. She returned after about a quarter of an hour and resumed her seat at the table.

'That was my father phoning from England. He is fairly high up in the Air Force and is working at the Ministry of Defence these days. He just said that something is going to happen tonight in Kampala but not to worry about it, just get home early and stay in your quarter for all of Sunday. We know about it in London and it's all for the best.'

We felt that we could not question her further on this news from her father, particularly as she had probably confided in us all that he had told her during the phone conversation. We finished the meal and I drove her back to the school quarters before calling in to share this strange piece of information with Sister Ita and the others.

The next morning we tuned into the World Service of the BBC and heard that a General Idi Amin had staged a military coup in Uganda and that tanks were on the streets of Kampala and at Entebbe Airport. In our part of Uganda the coup was greatly welcomed, and the Baganda dared to hope that the Kabaka might return from London to rule his kingdom again. The coup itself resulted in very few casualties in Kampala, and had the commander of a tank decided not to fire a shell at a portrait of Obote in the departure lounge of the National Airport at Entebbe then the coup might have been relatively bloodless in its early stages. As it was the effect of the shell bursting into a group of passengers waiting to board a flight to Europe caused several deaths and many severe injuries.

During those early days Idi Amin made several broadcasts to

the nation in English. One or two of the students in the local seminary came from the West Nile Region where Amin had his roots and knew that his command of English was poor. Furthermore, the content of the speeches gave the impression that these had been written for him and it transpired that two high-ranking British Army officers had flown into Kampala at about the same time as Obote was leaving for Singapore. One of these men had been Amin's commanding officer in the King's African Rifles many years previously, and whilst he was under their influence there was a strange 'honeymoon period' in Uganda. Within the last few years Dr Thomas Stuttaford, writing his regular column in *The Times*, mentioned a conversation that he had overhead between Sir Alec Douglas-Home, then Foreign Secretary, and Colonel Colin Mitchell (the hero of Aden a decade earlier) in the voting lobby of the House. Douglas-Home told Mitchell of the coup in Uganda, implying that this change for the better had been supported by Britain. Mitchell replied with some concern.

'Good Lord, Alec, I hope you know what you have done. I have met Idi Amin. It doesn't sound like a good swap to me.'

Within a few days Amin flew out by helicopter to visit all the main district centres, amongst which was Masaka, where he landed on the hill close to Kitovu Hospital. A big man with a wide smile and well turned out in his shirt-sleeve uniform, a military holster with pistol in his waistband and a forage cap, he cut a popular figure amongst the Baganda in those early days.

For the first few weeks after the coup many civil servants loyal to Obote were arrested and everyone was a bit 'edgy' because of the heightened level of security throughout Uganda. My sleeping pattern was even lighter than usual so I found myself wide awake one night at about three o'clock as I became aware that the veranda light had been turned on and a strange metallic noise was being made close to the main door. Cautiously I approached this intrusion and opened the front door. The night watchman was there in his First World War army greatcoat and black fedora hat, holding our dustbin lid and scraping up the heaps of flying insects that had been attracted to the veranda light. Sister Ita referred to him as the 'Watchnight', as she felt that this was a more accurate description of his perception of the job.

'What are you doing this for in the middle of the night?' I enquired of him.

'It is now the season of the flying grasshoppers and these are delicious to eat, so I am gathering them for my family.'

'Well, my family would like to have some sleep, so can you stop and gather this food some other time, please?'

Reluctantly he agreed to defer his food collection until the next night when he was due to be on duty at the hospital, but asked me to speak to the sisters.

'Please ask them to leave their outside lights switched on to attract the grasshoppers, as the season usually lasts for only a few nights.'

The following morning Fulgensio chuckled as I related this tale to him and explained that once the wings and the legs had been removed from these creatures they were fried in oil. Over mid-morning coffee Sister Ita confirmed that the creatures tasted just like shrimps when gathered fresh and fried, but few of us had the courage to follow her lead and try this seasonal dish. The following night we were again wakened by a noise on the veranda in the early hours and thinking that the relief night watchman was also improving his diet, I swung open the door to remonstrate with him. A large anteater, who had been hoovering up the grasshoppers, attracted in by the lights during the evening, gave me a quick glance before trundling off into the nearby banana plantation.

Fulgensio enlightened us about the many insects that were edible, and each had its season, sometimes only for only a few days. The seemingly inert termite heaps that dotted the landscape, sticking out like large dry fingers of hard-baked red clay, became very attractive when the time came for the young ants to fly out of the heap. The local children seemed to have the timing of the harvest down to a fine art. These metre-high columns were completely covered with a long cloth or an old blanket, and there the children waited. As the flight from the nest started, the immature ants were trapped and the children quickly peeled off the wings and ate them neat.

Some of the schoolchildren came to the front door and knocked timidly. They presented us with a little parcel of part of a banana leaf tied up with 'string' made from slivers of the bark of the tree. Fulgensio appeared silently on the scene.

'They wish to give you some of the termite grubs, Doctor, as the heaps are on your land.'

'Please thank them, Fulgensio, for their kind thought. Perhaps we will share them with the sisters.'

I am afraid that we did not even get as far as unwrapping the parcel, and Fulgensio was delighted to take them home with him.

'They are also especially good when fried in oil,' he confided to us as he left that evening.

The young banana leaf was utilised throughout that part of Uganda as tough clingfilm in which food, whether hot or cold, could be wrapped. In the rainy season many of the children walked to school clutching a banana leaf to hold off any sudden downpour. Held with the stalk just in front of the nose, the leaf allowed the rain to gather in the central spine and then run off the tip, hitting the ground about eighteen inches behind the holder's heels.

Most ants are capable of inflicting some form of sting or bite, and even a seemingly inert hard-baked termite heap will show some form of activity if it is sat upon for any length of time. The safari ants are high up the discomfort scale, with one of the most painful bites. Typically these are only seen after heavy rain when they decide to swarm about fifteen abreast over anything in their path. A dusty path or track suddenly has a thick moving black line running through it as thousands of these large black ants swarm to new territory.

The sisters were kind enough to ask me to read a lesson at their early morning mass on the feast day of St Luke, but I overslept by a few minutes. It was still dark as I closed the door of the bungalow as quietly as possible and then ran down 800 yards or so of track to the convent. Only on my return journey, when it was well light, did I realise that as a result of heavy rain in the night I had been running through a track of safari ants for many yards. I reached the convent chapel slightly out of breath but relieved to be in time for the lesson. A few minutes later I stood up to read the passage and felt sharp bites around my lower calf. As the lesson progressed the level of severe discomfort rose to the knee and then the mid-thigh. The speed of the reading increased greatly as I guessed that I was being attacked by numerous insects, and as I finished the passage the bites were already being felt in the groin.

I rushed to the outside door of the chapel and immediately took off my trousers and shook them hard to dislodge the offending ants. Dawn was just breaking over the sisters' little garden in front of the chapel and only as a sense of relief set in did I realise that two elderly Baganda women were kneeling in front of the statue of the Virgin in the middle of the garden. I put my trousers back on and returned to the chapel for the remainder of the Mass, but I obviously left two local ladies very confused about the behaviour of the doctor during the early morning Mass.

A few miles to the south the people living on the shores of Lake Victoria enjoyed a different seasonal form of protein when the tiny lake flies swarmed over the calm warm waters of this lake, which is roughly the size of Ireland. In Luganda these tiny flies, slightly smaller than the dreaded Scottish midge, were called *sami* and they gathered out on the lake to form huge swarms. Many of the local fishermen used to speak of them with great anxiety as there were instances of dug-out canoes being engulfed in large clouds of these tiny flying insects, resulting in severe breathing difficulties for the occupants who were unable to paddle fast enough to avoid the swarm. As these large grey clouds came into shore the local people gathered them in fine nets crafted out of thin cotton and the flies were then reduced to a paste which, according to one White Father, tasted not unlike fish paste.

The smallest of all the ants that we encountered in Uganda were the sugar ants. Any item of food containing even the smallest amount of sugar would be crawling with these tiny creatures if left out for more than a few minutes. Many of the older missions that we visited used to stand the table legs in cans of kerosene just to prevent ants from climbing up onto the table top.

John was in his early forties and was a schoolteacher who lived some thirty miles away from the hospital. He had been an insulin-dependent diabetic for five years before I arrived at Kitovu; his control had usually been good and he always kept his monthly check-up appointments. Then for two months in succession he failed to attend the hospital clinic. I discussed the problem with Sister Ita and she asked one of the local primary school teachers who knew John and his family. She obtained good directions from this friend for how to find him.

'It's a rough old road all right, but at least we are not in the rainy season so you should get through,' Sister Ita reassured me. 'John speaks good enough English so you will not need me along with you.'

A couple of days later I set off for John's village just as the schools were finishing for the day, and after just over one hour's drive I arrived in the village and was directed to his house.

Being the headmaster of the local primary school John's home was one of the more prestigious dwellings in the village; it was made of mud brick but with a corrugated iron roof and thus well protected from the seasonal heavy rains this made for a reliable form of construction. Inside there was a cement screed floor throughout, on which were placed locally woven mats and some sturdy furniture made from local hardwoods. The house was set in a *shamba* or homestead which comprised a banana plantation close to the road and then a collection of twenty to thirty coffee trees around the house itself along with orange and lemon trees. A great deal of coffee was grown by smallholders in this part of Uganda and for several weeks of the year the delicious perfume of the flowers on these small trees would permeate the house. Then, as the coffee berries took on their red hue and ripened, all the family would be involved in picking the coffee and drying it in the sun before bagging it and carting the sacks off to the local processing plant.

John was a little embarrassed to see me and even more self-conscious when he had to confess that he had given up the insulin for local medicine which seemed to be holding his diabetes under good control.

'It's a mixture of dried herbs that I have been buying from a local doctor (*muganga*) and she lives about forty miles from Kitovu Hospital in the direction of Kabale,' he explained. 'I continued with the insulin first of all and then reduced the dose as I felt the herb mixture was working well and now I have had no injections for a month.'

John promised to come to the hospital clinic for some blood tests and after some persuasion he agreed to take me to meet his *muganga* after this appointment.

'She specialises in diabetes and polio and is a very nice lady, and we can go to see her over half term.'

John's situation typified the problem experienced by many diabetic patients living in rural Uganda. Insulin-dependent diabetes was almost as common in Buganda as it was in Camberwell, but the disease was much more difficult to treat as many of the patients had no access to a refrigerator in which to store insulin. We tried to arrange access to a fridge at the local school or mission but these were often kerosene refrigerators and needed regular maintenance to ensure good temperature control. Add to this the difficulty in attending the hospital clinic on a regular basis with no reliable public transport and good diabetic control became almost impossible.

Two weeks later I set off from Kitovu with John to locate his *muganga*. She was a slightly built lady and was a good bit older than John. He greeted her with great respect and took her away to explain why he had brought along not only a total stranger, but also a foreigner. Using John as an interpreter she explained that she had carried on the family business from her father, who was a very good *muganga* and well known by the people for many miles around.

'Some of the very sick patients are admitted,' the old *muganga* explained. 'I have four rooms here to treat the patients who stay with me.'

Each patient attending, whether for a consultation or for admission, was asked to urinate against the doorframe on arrival. The density of the sugar ants which gathered around the specimen after ten minutes was an indication of the severity of the condition.

'The little ants are always accurate whatever time of the day the urine is passed,' she informed me. 'For new patients with many ants I start on the medicine (*dawa*) straight away. They receive three doses a day and must take no salt with the *dawa*.'

New patients spent a week with her before being sent home with medicine and thereafter they had to continue with morning and evening doses. She eventually agreed to sell me a reasonable quantity of the dried mixture from her store so that I could try using some in Kitovu. Whilst in her medicine store she could not resist showing me the special elixir that had been passed onto her by her father.

'This medicine can be taken by those older women who have to look after their grandchildren. When a young mother dies in childbirth and the small baby survives then it is the duty of the grandmother to raise that child. If she takes this medicine then her old breasts will start to produce milk again so that she can feed the baby.'

I recalled Sister Ita telling me of such grandmothers who were able to suckle these orphaned babies for a few months until the infant's system was mature enough to take cow's milk, and clearly a local herb gave this relationship a real chance of success.

This very experienced *muganga* then showed me her treatment centre for polio in a separate part of her homestead. All patients with polio were treated on a residential basis and she had accommodation for four patients (often teenagers with their mothers). From locally grown bamboo she had constructed parallel bars and walking frames.

'I have a special oil that I rub into their tight muscles and then I stretch their limbs,' she informed me with a little mime of her physiotherapy technique. 'Then they must exercise on the bars several times a day.'

I said farewell to this lovely old lady in my best Luganda and, clutching my sample of diabetic mixture, John and I returned to Kitovu, where I found – and paid for – a taxi to take John back to his home village.

The following week I sent a message with the Dennis Myanja, the hospital chaplain, to the bishop's office in the valley below the hospital. Knowing that Thomas, the head clerk at the parish house on the Sesse Islands, was a diabetic I suggested that he might like to come into hospital for a few days and try to come off his insulin injections. We admitted this thirty-year-old man a couple of weeks later and started him on the herbal mixture, at the same time reducing his dose of insulin and monitoring his blood sugar levels morning and evening. To our great surprise his control was well maintained and at the end of the week he left Kitovu to return to work with a supply of the medicine, along with instructions on how to find the *muganga* for further follow-up.

On a clear day we could see the Sesse Islands from the hill where the hospital was situated, and so when an invitation came some time later for us to spend a weekend with the White Fathers at the mission there we leapt at the opportunity. This group of islands lies just off the shore of Lake Victoria, and our enthusiasm for the weekend was a little tempered when we realised that a dug-out canoe was the only method of transportation, unless we had made a prior arrangement with the owner of a boat with an outboard engine. The distance involved did not seem too great, the lake was calm and the owner looked to be strong enough to paddle our family, so we boarded. The very construction of a dug-out means that passengers are seated well below the water line so one travels with a half-submerged feeling, but as we relaxed a little we took in the skills of the man paddling and the construction of his craft.

I was puzzled by a large stone in the bows which I felt added a little unreasonably to the weight, but thinking it was for ballast I asked the question: 'When do you use this stone?'

'Ah!' came the reply. 'I will have to use the stone there in case a hippo comes near the canoe. If I see him coming too close then I drop the stone on him and he goes away.'

Knowing the size and strength of a hippo and their reputation for being bad-tempered I hoped that we would not have to put this deterrent to the test.

We reached the island after a very good crossing and were met by Thomas, who immediately told us how well he was keeping on the *dawa* before leading us up the hill to the mission where we were introduced to the three White Fathers who were based there. The people living on the islands were Baganda and had moved from the mainland many years previously. Fishing was understandably the main industry and much of the fish caught was dried in the sun before being crated and shipped over to the mainland. With a cash income from this industry there was much less pressure to cultivate any surplus crops other than those needed to feed the family. As a result, much of the Sesse Islands at that time was still covered by tropical rainforest, and as we looked out from the windows of the mission the fathers pointed out the African Grey Parrots with their bright red tails high up in the trees.

On returning to Kitovu after the weekend I was fired with enthusiasm to gain some recognition for Uganda's herbs in providing the first oral treatment to replace insulin. I carefully packed up the remainder of the herbal mixture and posted the parcel to the head of the Diabetic Department at King's College Hospital in south London, indicating that I would soon be back on leave to discuss the matter with him in full detail.

As the children were growing up we decided to celebrate Easter in our second year by attending the midnight mass down at the cathedral. It was a very grand occasion, with the bishop himself presiding over the ceremonies with all the vestments, candles, incense and numerous innocent-looking boy acolytes dressed in spotless white surplices.

No one seemed to have realised that the East African Safari Rally was due to come through Masaka that evening. An ordinary motor parade would have stuck to the tarmac roads and caused no threat, but the very nature of this rally meant that they opted for the rough murram roads. The bishop was fairly well into the Easter liturgy when the ominous hum of the first car could be heard in the distance. As the engine noise came closer and louder many of the congregation were visibly distracted, but when the huge roar of power surged past the entrance road to the cathedral and whined off towards Masaka town many of the acolytes started to drift away. By the time the bulk of the rally came through the bishop had been deserted by all but the handful of priests assisting him and many of his congregation had shuffled out to watch the rally cars roar past. As we all wished each other a happy Easter in the early hours of the morning, the little altar boys were still wide-eyed with excitement, their white surplices covered with a film of red dust.

Meanwhile, other matters were causing the sisters some concern in the arena of family planning, where it appeared that herbal medicine had little to offer. Ever since I had arrived at Kitovu the sisters had allowed me to dispense contraceptive pills to the mothers who had large families and to women for whom another pregnancy would constitute a considerable risk. As the pill that we were using did not inhibit ovulation we benefited from permission given by a senior theologian at the University of Louvain to conduct a drug trial in rural Uganda with this progesterone only pill. The action of this pill thickened the mucus in the cervix and prevented sperm from gaining access into the uterus. As it was taken on a continuous basis, with none of the seven-day 'break' needed with the combined pill, it was good for compliance and our weekly clinic was attended by Catholic, Anglican and Muslim mothers alike.

Out of deference to the local Church authorities we did not advertise or promote the clinic. So when I returned from the Sesse Islands and Sister Ita informed me that the bishop would like to see me the next day to discuss this family planning clinic, we all feared that its closure would be imminent.

I duly presented myself, as requested, to the Bishop's House and after a few minutes was ushered into Bishop Ddungu's office. Mondays are usually a 'rest day' for the clergy, but here was the bishop immaculately turned out with a purple skull cap, purple piping on his cassock and purple silk socks. He rose from his chair and held out his hand, proffering the large episcopal ring which I kissed with a Luganda greeting. He returned the greeting but then immediately switched to English.

'Doctor Evans, thank you for coming to see me so promptly. How are your wife and your family?'

'Thank you, Bishop, they are all well. Sister Ita said that you wished to discuss something with me as soon as possible.'

'How is your work in the hospital?'

It is never the style in East Africa to rush the fences in any business matter. All the courtesies are exploited to the full and significant though the matter may be it is only addressed after a considerable preamble. After several more enquiries he moved to the matter in question.

' I believe you are holding a clinic in my hospital that helps mothers not to become pregnant?'

'That is true, Bishop, but we have obtained permission from a

Catholic University in Belgium to run a trial of this method and they send us the tablets.'

The fact that this conversation was taking place just three years after the publication of the highly controversial Papal Encyclical *Humanae Vitae* made me fearful that this service to many mothers with large families would be closed there and then.

'I have my sister staying with me but she is anxious to return home tomorrow; she lives in Kampala and she had a baby there three weeks ago.'

'I trust that they are both well and thriving, Bishop.'

'Indeed they are both well. But she is worried. She now has eight children and she is anxious not to have more children for some time. I have asked you to come to see me today as she would like to receive some of these tablets from you.' He paused. 'Would it be possible for you to see her later today, as she has to leave early tomorrow morning?'

I readily agreed to this suggestion and returned to Kitovu just as the sisters were meeting at the convent for the mid-morning break. I immediately allayed their anxiety about our clinic and pointed out to Sister Ita that one could almost say that the clinic had received a seal of approval. I walked back to the hospital with Sister Ita to resume my morning outpatient clinic, and as we walked through the patients' waiting area she nudged me and whispered:

'Would you ever look at that!'

She indicated a middle-aged lady wrapped in a large blanket. She was not local, and it subsequently turned out that she hailed from Kigezi in the south-west, where women were not permitted to smoke in public. She had a lighted cigarette inside her mouth, with just the filter tip visible around her pursed lips, and from her right ear little puffs of smoke were being emitted.

'She comes up here two or three times a year,' explained Sister Ita. 'She always likes a smoke whilst she waits – but with a perforated eardrum on that side she could do a wonderful party piece.' Sister Ita thought for a moment and then added 'Oh! By the way, there is a sister from Tanzania coming tomorrow to spend a few days with us. She is an obstetrician and gynaecologist like yourself and I am sure you would like to meet her.'

At teatime the following day I made my way to the convent and was introduced to Sister Maureen O'Mahoney, who had been working for the past ten years at a hospital run by the Medical Missionaries of Mary at Ndareda in northern Tanzania.

'I thought you might like to know, Richard, that a new teaching hospital is due to open in twelve months' time in Mwanza, on the southern shore of Lake Victoria. I have been offered a position there as Consultant in Obstetrics and Gynaecology, but my old pulmonary tuberculosis has become active again and I really cannot now accept the post.'

She went on to explain that this 600-bed hospital was being built with money donated by the Catholic Church in Germany but would be run and administered by the government of Tanzania. It was planned to include both a registered nurse and a medical assistant training school, and all patients would be treated free of charge.

'I was asking Sister Ita what your plans were when you finish here at Kitovu in three months' time,' Maureen mused, 'but she did not know and I just wondered if you were at all interested in taking my place in Mwanza in this exciting new venture.'

I asked Sister Maureen for some time to think it over. I had found Uganda and Kitovu so absorbing that I had given little thought about what to do next after my two-year contract was completed. At the back of my mind I had thought that two years working in a small mission hospital would get the bug of working in Africa out of my system and that I would return to a conventional post in the National Health Service back in England. The opportunity offered by this project in Tanzania was worthy of consideration for us as a family, and not least for Elizabeth, who had established a well-organised malnutrition clinic within the context of the maternal and child health service. But Tanzania (whose size roughly equates to half of the combined area of Western Europe) was a great challenge, being a much larger country than Uganda (whose area is roughly that of England and Wales combined). There were only two Tanzanian-qualified obstetricians and gynaecologists then serving a population of approximately 17 million, whereas Uganda, with its University Teaching Hospital in Kampala, had a Ugandan specialist in each of its thirteen district hospitals. The missions in the northern part of Tanzania were run by the White Fathers with whom we had enjoyed such a strong rapport in Uganda, so all things pointed us towards Mwanza. Sister O'Mahoney had given us the address of the medical superintendent at the hospital, so we wrote indicating our interest in taking the vacancy caused by her illness.

The end of our time at Kitovu came on all too quickly and we set about organising a party to say farewell to all the hospital staff, friends and the sisters. I discussed the menu with Fulgensio, pointing out that we had to cater for many different tastes, and about a fortnight before the event we were in the garden looking at our hens and ducks when up the drive from the hospital walked a pig. Nobody seemed to be following this pig or calling after it; it just trotted up our drive, with a length of banana fibre attached to one of its hind legs, where it had obviously broken the local bond of captivity. Then it stood still for a moment and grunted at us. I nudged Fulgensio, saying, 'I think we should try and catch this pig somehow.'

It was not an easy task as the pig had obviously made an recent escape and was not about to sacrifice his freedom without a struggle. Eventually we managed to corner the creature and, thanks to a rugby tackle from Fulgensio, we were able to tether him securely to a post where we left him overnight whilst we made enquiries. Fulgensio asked at the two local villages and I enquired of the sisters and all the hospital staff.

The sisters were kind enough to send up all the food leftovers from the convent and the hospital. Fulgensio fashioned a secure compound out of posts and wire but nobody in the local villages or the area around the hospital reported the loss of a pig. I suggested to Sister Ita that roast pork might be acceptable as a barbecue for our leaving party and she agreed that if the pig were still unclaimed by that date then Kagwire, the convent handyman, could organise the butchery business and the fire.

The guest list included nurses, laboratory staff, night watchmen, teachers and sisters, plus the hospital chaplain and the bishop. Kagwire started the evening in great form, supervising the fire and the cooking. Halfway through the evening he was hopelessly drunk, but by then the pig had been jointed and roasted to perfection. To everybody's surprise the bishop appeared when the party was in full swing and appeared delightfully relaxed; he mingled with all the other guests and seemed to enjoy the meal. His car and driver appeared after a couple of hours and I was chatting with Sister Ita as he came to take his leave.

'Thank you so much for such a wonderful party,' he enthused; 'it is a long time since I have tasted such tender pork. You know, I was given a pig a few weeks ago after a big confirmation at a nearby village, but as we reached the cathedral and opened the car door the pig escaped and it ran off, so we never saw it again.'

'Well I never,' volunteered Sister Ita. 'Perhaps it will come back to you, Bishop, one way or another.'

A few days later we boarded our Comet at Entebbe Airport for London, having left Karoli in the capable care of Eve Osborne, a lovely lady who had been the superintendent midwife at the Government Hospital in Masaka for many years and had adopted orphan triplets some five years previously. Karoli's father, aware of his own frail health and advancing years, had signed an official paper agreeing for us to adopt his son and raise him as our own, but official travel papers would take some time to finalise. It was also Eve who had found dear old Raffles for us, and, sensing that the dachshund was now too old to cope with the move to Tanzania, she offered to find a home for him. She knew of a young VSO nurse working in Masaka Hospital who would be delighted with the company of a well-trained dog.

We arrived back in England to find that Edward Heath, the Prime Minister, was completing the final stages of the negotiations that would see Britain become a part of the Common Market. On the world stage India was coping with a huge influx of refugees across its eastern borders as the civil war in East Pakistan moved towards the creation of the independent state of Bangladesh.

Once the opportunity presented itself, I contacted the head of the diabetic department at King's College Hospital to see if the herbal mixture had caused the anticipated medical breakthrough. I received the sobering report that the package had been impounded at Heathrow, having been found by sniffer dogs to contain traces of cannabis. The senior consultant did not wish to become involved in this sort of situation and so, denying all knowledge of me, suggested that the package be destroyed. I later learnt that all good local remedies throughout East Africa contain a touch of cannabis just to make the mixture more palatable to the patients.

# Chapter Five

After a hectic four weeks of visiting family and friends and stocking up on clothes and books, we flew back into Entebbe Airport just as the chilly evenings of autumn made the return to East Africa more attractive. We drove to Masaka to be reunited with Karoli who, with Eve's care and attention and the boisterous company of her triplets, had gained weight and confidence during our four-week absence. A departing Irish schoolteacher had gifted Eve their dog, as they felt it would fit in well with her family, but Eve had her doubts.

'I would be so grateful if you could include Sally in your party to Tanzania; she's a lovely dog but, with three active children, I really have my work cut out without further responsibilities, and she and Karoli get on so well together.'

Sally was a slim, lively mongrel, mainly black Labrador, and the children thought an instant dog was a good idea, so we packed up the estate car with our few belongings and then drove to Entebbe Port. We had booked cabins for the overnight journey on the RMV *Victoria* to Mwanza Port on the southern shores of Lake Victoria.

Two vessels provided the passenger and cargo service around Lake Victoria, plying between the Tanzanian ports of Bukoba and Mwanza in the west and south, the Kenyan port of Kisumu to the east and Entebbe. The SS *Usoga* was reputed to have started life as a fighting ship during the First World War when all the frames, steel plates and engine components had been transported overland before being assembled at Kisumu. The sight of her long single funnel, combined with a top speed of six knots conveyed an exact image of the early 1900s. The RMV *Victoria* was more modern and, fortunately, faster as well, but even so the fittings were all brass and hardwood in the cabins and a sedate air of luxury hung around the first-class accommodation.

The children watched with interest as the ship's crane loaded the car onto the freight deck and, whilst the family settled into our cabins for the overnight passage, I installed Sally in the car to act in her first capacity as our guard dog. The RMV *Victoria* sailed roughly on time from Kisumu and soon we were out into the open waters of Lake Victoria as the sun set quickly over the starboard side. A very pleasant meal was served in the restaurant, following which we organised the family into the two cabins for the night, and fortunately a calm voyage was to follow.

I woke the next morning just before dawn and went onto the deck to allow Sally to have a walk around before we went in for breakfast. One of the ship's officers commented on the dog and expressed the hope that I had the necessary paperwork to import the animal into Tanzania. This came as a complete shock, as I was under the impression that since the three countries had been formed into an East African Community then the passage of domestic pets presented no problem. He advised me that this was not the case and that certainly various veterinary certificates would have to be produced. I decided there and then that the best way to cope with this problem was to open the door of the car just before it was offloaded. This would allow Sally to roam free in the hope that she had probably got to know us well enough to follow us through the port buildings and rejoin us on the outside. It was certainly my impression that the ports of Kigoma and Entebbe were so busy when a ship docked that along with several dogs roaming around the port area in amongst the hordes of people who were meeting, greeting or travelling, then our dog would certainly evoke no interest.

Mwanza Port was already in sight over the bow of the ship and the morning was crystal clear, with a glassy calm lake. As we neared Mwanza the huge rocky outcrops and large boulders around the lakeshore became much more obvious and these were interspersed with large green areas of papyrus reeds. Some of these, I later learnt, were floating islands that would detach themselves from one part of the lakeshore when the wind changed, only to find another resting place further down the shore. Gone were the green banana plantations and the luxuriant vegetation around the shore. Even though this was obviously the same altitude as Entebbe in Uganda, Tanzania felt hotter and drier, and appeared from the ship's deck to be more arid.

At that time in late 1971 Tanzania was listed by the World Bank as the poorest country in Africa. It is larger than twice the size of the state of California in the USA, and the mainland part of Tanzania had been independent since 1961. In 1964 Tanganyika merged with Zanzibar to form the United Republic of Tanzania, and Julius Nyerere was elected president of the new republic, a position that he was to hold with great honour and integrity until he decided to retire in 1985.

I had made the decision to leave Uganda, with its university medical school of Makerere and its infrastructure of Ugandan specialists in each of its twelve regional hospitals. In 1971 Tanzania had only three consultant obstetricians and gynaecologists in the entire country; the senior of these three was a delightful man with whom I had worked at Plymouth some five years previously, so I looked forward to renewing our friendship again. Tito was based in Dar es Salaam at the newly established University Medical School where he was head of the department of obstetrics and gynaecology.

Outside the capital city the medical services were patchy and often underfunded. Two large missionary organisations, one Catholic and the other Protestant, had each agreed to build a new teaching hospital to serve the large populations in the north-west and the north-east of Tanzania respectively. The Protestant organisation had built the Kilimanjaro Christian Medical Centre, whilst the Roman Catholic organisation had built the new Mwanza Teaching Hospital. It was this new eleven-storey hospital that was now clearly visible on a hill above the town, looking down onto the port area where we were now docking. Both of these church organisations were based in West Germany, but obviously funds were brought in from all over Europe. Each of the hospitals was built and equipped through voluntary contributions, on the understanding that once completed the Ministry of Health in Dar es Salaam would take over the running costs and future funding. It was further agreed that there would be a two-year spell during which time the senior expatriate staff would endeavour to hand over responsibilities to the local Tanzanian employees of the Ministry of Health. All patients would thus be treated free of charge both for outpatient and inpatient services, along with any medication needed.

The RMV *Victoria* was met at Mwanza Port by John, the English hospital secretary, and his wife Barbara, who had just started work as the senior laboratory technician. They had arrived in Tanzania some six months earlier after working in a large hospital in northern Nigeria in similar roles. Having explained to John about the difficulty of Sally, who was still following me, John and I walked through the immigration and customs area together, doing our best to ignore the dog. Sure enough, Sally followed a few paces behind us as we left the port buildings, equally happy to be on terra firma, and waited patiently for the car to be offloaded. Our estate car was eventually unloaded and our belongings packed into the back, along with Sally, before Elizabeth drove the vehicle out of the port area. We were then taken to our home, which turned out to be a new house in a block of five just outside the main hospital compound but overlooking Mwanza Port and the lake. This staff housing complex, built to a very high specification, was designed for the senior staff with families, and smaller staff units were also provided on the other side of the access road to the hospital for staff who were single or had no children.

The following day we accompanied John and Barbara on a tour of the new hospital, which was structurally just complete but needed a further three to four months of work to fit all the equipment and connect all the plumbing and electricity. We were introduced to the American medical superintendent, who had arrived in Tanzania a few months earlier and was also a specialist in obstetrics and gynaecology. Bill was delighted that we had arrived, as he would now be able to give more of his energy and time to fitting out the hospital and interviewing senior Tanzanian staff whilst I took over the clinical duties at the old hospital in the town with its outpatient centre.

This hospital had been built around the turn of the century by the German colonial power when Tanzania was Deutsch-Ostafrika. Many of the original buildings remained and these were constructed with either mud and wattle walls or a baked mud brick construction, often with locally made pantiles on the roof. Sanitation and lighting were poor throughout the hospital and overcrowding was a great problem, with patients often sleeping on mattresses on the floor between the beds. Much of the equipment was in a very poor condition and drug availability was limited, whilst medical supplies were erratically maintained. After the well-ordered hygiene of Kitovu this was a new and strange world, for which I was ill-prepared. The outpatient clinic, some half a mile away from the hospital, was a newer building and was named after one of the West African leaders, Sekou Tourre. By contrast, this was a well-maintained and well-planned clinic, but each morning it served as the only medical centre for the great majority of the town's population and only when this workload had been addressed could specialist clinics then take place in the afternoons.

Tanzania at that time was far more unified than either Kenya or Uganda, the other two members in the East African Community. Whilst it was obviously the 'poor cousin' of the three countries it was fiercely proud of its independent status, and this was manifest in the importance given to the national language of Kiswahili. Kenya had a huge expatriate population, many of them landowners and businessmen in their own right, and English was widely spoken throughout the country. Uganda also had a sizeable expatriate population and English was both the language of commerce and also widely used by young Ugandan Asians, as it was the smart language to speak. Arriving in Tanzania I was immediately stuck by the importance given to Kiswahili; all new expatriate staff of the hospital were encouraged to attend evening classes twice a week to learn the language. These sessions were run by a charming and experienced teacher from one of the local secondary schools, and these classes also afforded the opportunity to get to know other new colleagues on the project.

All these new members of staff had previous experience in Africa, generally in voluntary agency or mission hospitals, and thus for us all the experience of working on a government contract was new. All expatriate staff, therefore, received salaries on the same scale as a Tanzanian government civil servant, but the founding organisation (Miserior) agreed to top up the salaries of married staff with family commitments for the first five years. Our Kiswahili instructor was at pains to inform us of the privileged position accorded to our group of medical expatriates by the virtue of being government employees. He pointed out that this gave us our own position in the infrastructure of this strongly socialist country.

One of the immediate differences between Tanzania and its northerly neighbours in East Africa was the quality of the roads. There was a limited amount of tarmac road in Mwanza, but this quickly ended about seven or eight miles out of the town and from then on rough murram roads continued until one reached Tabora, 210 miles to the south, or Arusha, 250 miles to the east. Whilst the murram roads in Uganda and Kenya were fairly level and well maintained, the vast size of Tanzania, and the limited amount of money available for road maintenance, meant that the majority of the roads were rutted and uneven, often with large potholes. A Land Rover was the most reliable way of getting around the region, and our estate car with its soft suspension was clearly not suitable. John and Barbara had purchased a good second-(or third-) hand Land Rover from an Asian garage owner on the outskirts of the town and a quick phone call organised an appointment for me to meet him.

Julie, as he was known to all the hospital community, was a short, wiry individual with an excellent command of English and a delightful sense of humour. He informed me that my Ugandan-registered car would be liable to import duty if I chose to keep it in Tanzania and thus my decision to go for a Land Rover was sensible from both the financial and the mechanical point of view. Through the Ismaili network he contacted a friend of his in Kampala who agreed to buy my Toyota estate once Julie had given him all the details over the telephone and described the condition of the car. Julie seemed more than happy to credit me with the sale price agreed with his Ugandan friend in Tanzanian shillings, as officially the three currencies in Uganda, Kenya and Tanzania at that time stood at parity. In my naïve way I thought that the car would be loaded on to the RMV *Victoria* again and would make its way back to Uganda, but Julie had other ideas. He knew a Kenyan driver who would take the car over the border into Kenya and then drive through the western part of Kenya and so into Uganda. Both border crossings would be made at night when the Customs Officers were more amenable to conducting unofficial business. Julie then arranged a changeover date for the vehicles in order to give himself time to finish the work on the Land Rover and early the following week I drove the Toyota estate car to Julie's garage, left it with him and drove away in the Land Rover.

The following morning I drove my robust Land Rover into the hospital car park in time for a teaching ward round with the pupil midwifes. These young nurses behaved rather strangely, with much giggling and furtive whispering, plus a few sidelong glances. Eventually I asked the reason for the continuous little distractions. One of the more forward of the pupil midwives spoke for the group.

'Are you feeling all right this morning, Doctor?'

'Yes thank you. I am very well. Why?'

'Well, you see, Doctor, your car was parked outside the Kitenge Bar for many hours last night and we thought you must be very tired.'

This Kitenge Bar, I was to learn later, was one of the most notorious whorehouses in Mwanza. The driver of my car, having been paid cash in advance, decided to spend both his time and his money enjoying the delights of the Kitenge Bar until he set off on his journey around one o'clock in the morning. This would allow him to reach the border with Kenya at about 3 a.m. Many of the pupil midwives were socialising in the town that evening, and seeing my car parked outside this particular location for such a long time they attributed to me a degree of notoriety and stamina that was not fully deserved. In order that the ward round might continue with a little more attention being paid, I took them to the window and showed them my recently acquired Land Rover and explained that my distinctive estate car was no longer in my possession, nor in the country any more. This message took some time to filter down and I continued to receive sidelong glances and giggles in hospital corridors for several days after the transfer.

A far greater diversion took place in March 1972 when the official opening of the hospital took place, and for this event President Nyerere was not only the guest of honour but also responsible for opening the impressive new hospital.

Julius Nyerere was a man of small stature but great intellect and enormous charisma. He had studied at Edinburgh University before returning to colonial Tanzania as a teacher in the run-up to independence. His lasting claim to fame among his fellow teachers, was that he translated the major works of Shakespeare into Kiswahili. He entered politics in the late 1950s and was duly elected president of Tanganyika at Independence on 7th July 1961. He and his family are members of one of the smallest of the 120 or so tribes in Tanzania, and his tribal homeland was some 100 miles east of Mwanza. This meant that many of his family (brother, mother, aunt and nephews) came to Mwanza Hospital on several occasions during the five years that I was working there. At no time was any fuss or privilege ever sought, even on the two or three occasions the President himself paid a private visit to members of his families who were ill.

The hospital opening ceremony was similarly low key and was not accompanied by any of the oppressive security or motorcades so characteristic of most African presidents. The presidential car was preceded by one police car and a security Land Rover. Nyerere was relaxed and informal throughout the time that he was at the hospital, equally at ease with both Tanzanian party workers, officials and expatriate staff. His manner with both the patients and the many children who attended the ceremony was one of unhurried concern. I was subsequently presented to President Nyerere on three or four occasions during the years that I worked in Tanzania and I found that provided you opened the conversation courteously and confidently in Kiswahili then he would quickly switch to English to put you at your ease.

The high spot of the day's celebrations after the official opening of the hospital was provided by the Sukuma drummers and snake dancers. The Sukuma is the largest tribe in Tanzania, living in the lands on the southern shores of Lake Victoria and extending some 100 miles to the south. These people hold snakes in high regard, viewing them as the spirits of their ancestors and therefore seldom killing them without great provocation. In the forecourt of the new hospital young men danced with coils of large pythons entwined around their bodies, to the rhythmic pounding of the huge Sukuma ceremonial drums, which often measure five feet in diameter. The pythons were never held in permanent captivity but were released to the swampy foreshore area around the lake after any dancing ceremony. From here they would emerge once every two or three weeks in search of food, sometimes dogs or even goats, sliding through the lakeside villages in the late evening. Sometime after the opening ceremony of the hospital I was driving back home to the hospital in the middle of a tropical storm just after dusk. I was negotiating the heavy rain and potholes of a lakeside track in my newly acquired Land Rover, when I saw the road ahead blocked by a fallen tree. I slowed down in order to drive over this obstacle when I realised that the 'tree' was actually moving. After what seemed like an age it tapered and the thin tail of the huge python then cleared the road as it continued in its search for a meal in the height of the storm.

Alongside the Sukuma reverence for snakes a number of official snake charmers existed, and these formed an elite group of men and women who made pets not of the huge pythons but of the smaller, and much more deadly, cobras and mambas. I first came across one of these snake charmers when I noticed a very old van in the hospital car park with the windows down, and a complete disregard for security. Closer inspection showed the coils of a large cobra on the passenger seat and I immediately backed away from the vehicle, to the great amusement of the uniformed attendant on the hospital gate. He explained to me: 'This car belongs to a snake charmer and no thieves will dare to try and steal the car with that on the front seat.'

'How on earth does the snake charmer manage not to get bitten himself?'

'Ahh! Doctor, you see each time that this man has to cut his own fingernails, because they are growing too long, then he also cuts the fangs of his snakes and with his fingers he milks the mouth of the snake.'

Clearly the technique here was to ensure that the fangs are kept blunt and the venom sacks are kept milked at regular intervals, but it would be a courageous stranger who assumed that these procedures had been recently performed and that the snake on the driving seat was therefore totally harmless.

The compound around the new family houses had its own local population of reptiles. As several areas of the large boulders that so characterised the Mwanza landscape remained close to the houses, it was in this refuge that the reptiles lived whilst the houses were being built and in the days of our early occupation. We soon became aware that the large group of rocks near to our house was the home of a large monitor lizard, some five feet in length, and fortunately very shy in nature. He would usually emerge at around midday to bask in the heat of the sun but always retreated whenever either our children or the local village lads were moving around. A puff adder and a spitting cobra were also encountered during those early months but fortunately without any aggression; they very quickly moved off into the dry dusty terrain of the garden and beyond. We were advised that planting some trees would lessen the risk of the snakes taking up residence around the house, and the local forestry department provided healthy small trees at a very low cost, so eucalyptus and citrus were purchased.

One or two reptiles break the rule of preference for a dry habitat, and the appearance of a black bootlace snake in the upstairs bath convinced us that some reptiles at least prefer a dark damp pipe. The hospital engineer kindly provided some metal mesh with which to cover the outlet pipes and I set to work to ensure that the three or four drainage pipes would not provide access into the house for further reptiles. Our main drainage pipe seemed to develop increasing problems with intermittent blockages, and I attempted to rod out the obstruction, with no success. The site of the blockage seemed to be just after the U-bend in the kitchen sink, and I disconnected the nearest junction and shone a torch in to investigate. Two large eyes looked back at me. On closer inspection it was fairly obvious that a toad had crawled up into the pipe backwards and had now become wedged at the first bend. I managed to use two dessert spoons in the manner of obstetric forceps, lubricated with KY jelly, and managed to get the spoons on either side of this poor toad's jaw before delivering him out of his prison.

The new hospital had opened and the intense overcrowding and poor hygiene in the old hospital had given way to spacious wards and impressive facilities in the large new building. But after a few weeks we were all aware that this new hospital was to offer its facilities and services not just to Mwanza town but to the whole of the north-west of Tanzania. It was decided therefore that small teams of consultants would visit the regional centres to spend time with the medical officers and staff there and explain to them the services that were offered in Mwanza. This would call for a certain degree of diplomacy, as the Tanzanian regional medical officers had been running the hospitals in their regions reasonably effectively in the decade or so of independence.

I was to be part of a team that would visit Bukoba in the far north-west of the country, and also Kigoma in the mid-west, situated on the shores of Lake Tanganyika. Other teams would visit Musoma on the eastern shore of Lake Victoria close to the Kenyan border, and Tabora, some 150 miles to the south of Mwanza. We were to meet the regional medical officer and as many of his medical staff as was possible and explain to them the facilities that were offered in Mwanza and the most appropriate groups of patients that could be referred to this new regional centre. My first trip was to Bukoba, and as this is a port on the western shore of Lake Victoria close to the border with Uganda, we made the trip by lake steamer, sailing from Mwanza at around noon, and arriving in Bukoba the following morning.

We found the town of Bukoba to be very 'on edge', as hostility was rapidly growing between Tanzania and Uganda at that time and Bukoba was only a few miles from the Ugandan border. Milton Obete had returned to East Africa and, joined by his wife and several of his ex-ministers, had taken refuge in Dar es Salaam as a guest of President Nyerere. Idi Amin viewed this hospitality with great suspicion and immediately declared the Tanzanian president and the people of Tanzania to be enemies of Uganda. He suspected, probably with some foundation, that Obete was gathering a force of Ugandan expatriates, sundry mercenaries and possibly some Tanzanian troops to invade Uganda and reinstate himself as president. The police and the very strong army presence in Bukoba were clearly on the lookout for any Ugandans crossing the border bent on sabotage or espionage. Our small party of four specialists included a psychiatrist, who was not only a Tanzanian but also came from the Sukuma tribe, and was very good company. Sam led us into the Lake Hotel and, as he had stayed there before, he arranged single rooms for each of the four of us. I was the second one after Sam to sign the hotel register and the pleasant girl at the reception desk looked up and asked me:

'Do you require central heating?'

I turned to Sam and said, 'It seems very hot here at this time of year; surely we have a translation problem here, it cannot be central heating.'

Sam chuckled and whispered to me 'That means "Do you want one of the hotel's girls in your room at night?"'

I politely declined this offer of the hotel's extra facilities.

The following morning we had a full tour of the regional hospital in Bukoba and met many of the staff, and also had a chance to look at the wards and the operating facilities. The value of Sam's presence in our team was further underlined when he was made aware, on a very informal basis, that a number of patients were being held in the cells of the local police station. Sam indicated that would like to see these patients who were being held in custody, as important medical considerations might be involved in their detention. As the local police were answerable to the military authorities it was only after considerable discussion that we were allowed access to the police cells, and only at the very last minute were the three expatriate specialists allowed to accompany Sam into the cells.

A strange assortment of half a dozen patients were being held; two were Ugandan nationals and two were refugees from neighbouring Rwanda. Even with Sam's Kiswahili and psychiatric training it was very difficult to converse with these four individuals and so our attention was turned to a fifth patient who was held in solitary confinement in the strongest cell of all. On looking through the peephole in the door we saw a very well built man in his mid-thirties sitting in the corner of the cell. All his clothes had been removed and he held in his right hand a huge erection in the manner of a portable microphone. This poor disturbed individual had been in this state for the past three days with a continuous erection and he was in deep conversation with Idi Amin, through his member, so that all the local militia were convinced that he was a spy and a threat to national security. After some discussion Sam eventually persuaded the local commander to release this patient into our care on condition that we would take him back to Mwanza under sedation and fully clothed. Sam then signed the police discharge book which still listed the patient as a 'dangerous spy' rather than a schizophrenic.

One month later I was on the move again as a member of a similar team of specialists, this time visiting Kigoma, the regional town to the south-west of Mwanza on the shore of Lake Tanganyika. It was near here that Stanley had met Livingstone over 100 years earlier, but our journey was far less arduous. We boarded a train in Mwanza at eight o'clock in the morning and headed out for the direction of Dar es Salaam. We steamed due south for most of the day, reaching the old German administrative capital of Tabora in the late afternoon. Here we changed trains and, leaving our mainline train to complete a further twenty hours of travel to its destination of the present capital on the Indian Ocean, we boarded a connecting train on the branch line to Kigoma and were soon steaming west into the setting sun.

I left the stuffy heat of the compartment and stood in the corridor by a door with the window down. The warm air rushed in as we gathered speed and soon I was joined by a railway guard who pointed out the impressive avenue of mango trees that lined the main road from Tabora to Kigoma, which at that time ran alongside the railway.

'Those trees,' he informed me, 'grew from mango stones thrown away by the slaves as they were marched from Kigoma down to the coast where they were to be sold.'

He then went on to point out other geographical features and the interesting parts of the journey that lay ahead.

'Soon we will leave this road and we then cross the marshes where we can sometimes buy very good fish,' he confided.

A train in East Africa, like trains in many developing countries of the world, forms a huge sales opportunity for those isolated communities living alongside the rail track. At any station, level crossing or watering stop, a variety of fruits, home-made doughnuts and roasted peanuts were offered through the windows. Live chickens, eggs and vegetables, along with seasonal fruits, were sold to the restaurant car. Some of the passengers travelling on top of the third-class carriages had the privilege of being able to buy items of livestock, mainly chickens and goats, as long as they were transported with them on top of the carriage and not inside it. These railside purchases involved a great deal of haggling and I was amazed at how quickly an agreement could be reached once the train's whistle had sounded and a head of steam had driven the huge engine wheels into a couple of revolutions forwards.

My friendly guard continued his chatter.

'I really like the run to Dar es Salaam,' he said, 'because I then have two days off after the journey and I can go to the cinema and watch some of those American films. Kumbe! Those film stars and the sacrifices they make.'

'They are paid well for it,' I said, thinking of how his weekly wage would compare to Hollywood film stars' income.

'Ahh,' replied the guard, 'what is the use of money to their widows and family after such a film?'

I now caught the drift of this conversation and where it was heading and so I attempted to convince him that the actors did not really die, but everything was achieved by special effects and acting. The last film that he had seen in Dar es Salaam was *The Wild Bunch*, and so he was adamant.

'Don't tell me they didn't die. I saw the bullets go in. The wounds; the blood, Kumbe! What a sacrifice!'

The first call for dinner ended our conversation.

After a good meal, and a bottle of Dodoma red wine, we made our way to the two tier bunks in the sleeping compartment and, in spite of all the rattling and swaying, managed to get to sleep until a sudden jolt woke me with a start at about four o'clock in the morning. I then had a strange feeling that we were going backwards through the night, and I eased out of the bunk without waking the Dutch surgeon above me and walked out into the corridor. My friendly guard was near the same door where we had talked earlier.

'Why are going backwards now? Is anything wrong?'

'Yes. We have lost some fish,' came the unexpected reply. 'You see, if the engine crew buy fish then it is too hot for them to keep the fish there so they fix it to the buffers.'

Looking out through the open door I saw two other railway staff searching the tracks ahead of the last coach as the train eased slowly backwards and with the help of the powerful light they were scanning the sleepers between the tracks.

'The driver bought some very good fish a few miles back when we crossed the swamps and he tied them to the buffers in front but they seem to have dropped off. So we are going back to look for them.'

Another five minutes of slowly reversing into the night resulted in the fish being found and happily they were undamaged. They were retied to the front buffers, a little bit more securely this time, and we proceeded on our way to Kigoma. We must have made up time because we arrived on schedule and found Kigoma looking very impressive in the early morning light reflected off a calm lake. This was the area where the tsetse fly, the carrier of sleeping sickness, was still common, and my strongest memory of that hospital visit was the ward full of patients, victims of this incurable disease.

The last of the outreach programmes took me, again as a part of a team of four, to the town of Musoma on the eastern shores of Lake Victoria. This was a journey by road and, as there were special maternal and child health interests in the area, it was an opportunity to take our own Land Rover with Elizabeth and the children. Elizabeth was rapidly building up an interest and an involvement in the rural clinics devoted to maternal and child health and had received an invitation from the community nurse on the island of Ukerewe to pay them a visit. My visit to Musoma with the team was therefore shortened and, after a brief tour of the hospital and an introduction to the staff, I made my apologies and left with the family for the island of Ukerewe just south of Musoma.

This island was separated from the mainland by a sheltered channel, and we did not have to wait long for the flat pontoon ferry to arrive at the small terminal there to transport us across. The weather looked very ominous, with huge black thunder clouds brewing up over the horizon as we joined the three other vehicles on this ferry. There was the usual delay in casting off as loads of luggage had to be brought on and stowed, but eventually we loosed our moorings and the heavy diesel engine started up for the thirty-minute crossing to Ukerewe Island. The storm continued to approach with what seemed like great speed and we were very relieved that we had chosen to cross to the island by sheltered channel rather than a trip on the open lake.

I then became aware of a stirring among the African passengers, who were finding it very difficult to control their laughter and remain polite to us at the same time. They were looking at the children, who were standing on the iron plates of the ferry deck. I saw what was captivating everybody else's attention. Both Claire's long blonde hair and Jonathan's shorter blond hair were standing right up on end. Clearly this was a problem that was affecting all family members; the high level of static electricity in the air caused by the approaching electrical storm had made us all look like a primary school drawing of Ken Dodd. Once we understood what was causing the mirth of our fellow passengers we were able to join in and even try to get each other's hair to settle down against the electrical impulses. We arrived at Ukerewe Island just as this huge thunderstorm broke, and we drove the fifteen minutes or so to the hospital through heavy rain, blinding flashes of lightning and huge thunder claps. As we arrived in the hospital we were alerted to the fact that a young woman had just been brought in from a nearby village with the story that she had been struck by lightning. I went in to the casualty unit there and saw this young woman with no heartbeat and a burn running down from her right shoulder over her right hip to her right ankle in a characteristic fern-like pattern.

We established an airway and then, with the help of two of the local staff, we started resuscitation attempts. Happily, her heart restarted after the first four hard thumps of cardiac massage, and within a few minutes she was breathing. Some ten minutes later she became conscious, although a little bit dazed and confused.

We stayed overnight at Ukerewe Island and so I was able to visit her the next day on the ward where she was slowly regaining the use of her right arm and leg. She remembered very little about the lightning strike, but certainly her heart would have suffered no permanent damage. A cardiac arrest occurring during a lightning storm in a young person is often the result of a heavy electrical discharge interrupting the normal conducting system of the heart. Prompt action of external cardiac massage is usually successful in restarting the heart, and it is one of the few occasions where this form of resuscitation can be rewarding.

We visited some of the maternal and child health clinics on the island, and then we made a short trip on a crowded local boat to the island of Ukara, just off the northern shore. All the clinics on this small but highly fertile island were well run, with great motivation of the staff, in spite of the very poor facilities and supplies.

Just before leaving to catch the return ferry to the mainland, this time on a clear sunny afternoon with not a cloud in the sky, I called in to the hospital to see the lady who had been struck by lightning and found that she was sitting up in bed and anxious to return home. A slight commotion in the casualty unit caught my attention and I went in to see what was happening. The male staff nurse explained to me:

'This man has come from a village five miles away on the lakeshore and he is very anxious.'

Certainly this assessment of the man's state of mind was accurate, as the forty-year-old man appeared very agitated and probably incoherent even to those who understood the language better than I did.

'He says that last night his right shoe was taken and he is very afraid for his life,' continued the nurse. 'You see, it could well have been taken by his enemies and given to their crocodile.'

I expressed some confusion as to how crocodiles should have entered into a situation regarding the loss of this man's personal property. The nurse then informed me:

'Ahh! There are many crocodiles in the lake around here and some people have been able to train them so that if they give them a shoe or some clothing of their enemy then the crocodile will come to that person's house in the night and take him away into the lake.'

Clearly the people of Ukerewe Island have been living with crocodiles for hundreds of years, rather like the Sukuma with the snakes, but I was surprised to learn that they could be trained in this way. I left the nurse advising the man to buy himself another pair of shoes and go and stay with some relatives on the other side of the island for a few days.

My first night back on duty after the Ukerewe safari was interrupted by a call at three o'clock in the morning. I knew from my ward round the previous evening that we had a mother of twins in labour, but with the first baby coming as a normal head presentation, I hadn't expected any great problems, especially as our midwifes were so competent at handling twin deliveries.

'It is the labour ward, Doctor, we have a problem.'

'Is it the twin mother? Is there a problem with her?'

'Oh no. It is not the patient; it is the Indian doctor. He has fainted away.'

I then realised that a recently arrived junior doctor, a graduate from a South India medical school, did not have any great experience in obstetrics and therefore he was finding the position a bit of a sharp learning curve. I went over to the hospital and to the obstetric department, where I found this young man was just coming round on a rather messy labour ward floor. I sent him off to bed and waited for the twin mother to deliver her second baby. Later that day, after the morning ward round, I questioned him and he confessed that he had never seen a baby born before and the experience was too much for him. Closer questioning then revealed that he had qualified as a mechanical engineer but he could find no work in that field in South India. He therefore paid for a forged medical graduation certificate and sent it off to the Ministry of Health in Dar es Salaam so that he arrived in Tanzania as a medical doctor. After the experience of the previous night he was happy to be suspended with immediate effect and return to India. From then on the Ministry of Health took much more care in authenticating the certificates of young doctors coming to work from the Indian subcontinent.

Whether it was this event or whether it was the success of our outreach programmes and the increased numbers of patients being referred to us from the regional centres we did not know, but at the end of that first year we received recognition from the University Medical School in Dar es Salaam for the training of interns. We were now assured of locally trained Tanzanian doctors to be posted to work in the new hospital at Mwanza.

## Chapter Six

An invitation for our family to go and spend a weekend with English doctors at a private hospital some eighty miles south of Mwanza was an unexpected spin-off from the large regional outreach programme. The medical officer in charge of the hospital at Mwadui, just outside Shinyanga, had a special interest in anaesthetics whilst his wife, also a qualified doctor, was interested in maternal and child health. John had three patients who needed major gynaecological surgery whilst Anna was anxious to sit down with Elizabeth and plan maternal and child health outreach programmes from the rather sealed and sterile atmosphere of the private hospital.

As they had three children of similar ages it seemed an ideal opportunity to combine business with pleasure over a weekend. The first evening of our stay we heard the extraordinary story of how the diamonds in this area had been discovered. J T Williamson was a young prospector wandering around the northern part of Tanzania between the two world wars and, realising that many of the rock formations around Shinyanga were associated with possible diamond deposits, he booked into a small hotel in the town. After several fruitless days of prospecting and searching he came back with one or two small diamond fragments and was looking at these one evening over a glass of beer in the local hostelry. A cattle herder on the next table leaned over and through an interpreter said that he knew just where stones like these could be found, only much larger. Williamson accompanied the man and his cattle out of town the next day and was shown large alluvial diamonds in the loose stones at the foot of the small hilly outcrops some thirty miles from Shinyanga. So started a large and profitable diamond mine at Mwadui, and as a lasting form of recognition a large bronze statue of Williamson, dressed in his prospecting gear, was erected right in front of the main administrative building.

As we were shown around the following morning Jonathan's eyes alighted on this marvellous, rugged piece of art, and as the only statues he had ever seen were religious ones in churches he asked: 'Why is God wearing such big boots?'

The senior security officer at the mine subsequently told me that once or twice a year this old cattle herder would appear at the front entrance with his herd of long-horned cattle and present his compliments to Mr Williamson. It was always understood that two or three security guards would then be detailed to watch over the cattle while this man was ushered in to the private compound, taken to the officers' mess and given whatever he wished to drink.

With such a valuable export commodity being mined in an area of such poverty the security around the mine was understandably very tight. Throughout my time in Mwanza numerous local employees in the hospital would approach me, often in the seclusion of a lift or a washroom, offering me diamonds at a cut price. Had I expressed an interest I would probably have been shown glass chips from old Coca-Cola bottles, but all the expatriate hospital staff were cautioned not to entertain thoughts of immediate wealth by buying into such offers.

Family life in Mwanza for the whole of the five years that we spent there was made much more comfortable by the presence of a farm run by a Swiss family on the shores of the lake. This whole business was then run by Mrs Gaetje, an impressive matriarch, who had been in Tanzania since German colonial times and had a great understanding and rapport with the local farmers. She had organised a system whereby milk was collected early each morning from a number of farmers with milking herds and brought to her farm where it was put through a pasteurising plant before being bagged into half-litre units. These were then taken over the gulf on her ferry to Mwanza town and sold from her dairy shop. She managed to make butter two or three times each month and this also appeared for sale on her counter. In addition she carried a range of fresh vegetables, eggs, and pork.

She also had built three or four cottages in the very attractive lakeshore gardens close to her own house in which visitors were accommodated. It proved to be a special treat for the children to spend a weekend in one of these cottages, in spite of the presence of a tame pelican called Percy who took to following the children around clacking his large bill in order to be fed any titbits. The only way to get Percy to move on was to grip him by the tip of his (closed) bill and then lead him away to the lakeside; as the children were too short to execute this manoeuvre, they lived in constant dread of the bird's approach.

The lakeshore around this development had been kept clear of the small snails and the vegetation on which they depended, so it was the only area on the lakeshore that was probably free from bilharzia. The parasite responsible for this disease divides its time between water snails and human beings. The parasite is discharged by the snails and then contaminates fresh water. The small parasitic worms pass into humans through the skin of the feet and legs when walking or swimming in lake water and quickly pass into the veins to take up residence around the lower gut and bladder. After the initial infection, which is characterised by a fever with nausea, abdominal pain and rashes, the real problems start to develop in the bladder and bowel, and only recently has an effective treatment been developed for this very debilitating disease.

The pattern of life in Mwanza town and the new hospital was abruptly shattered at five o'clock one October morning in 1972 when a single Ugandan military aircraft flew over Lake Victoria before turning to drop a stick of bombs on the sleeping town. Mercifully more than half of these high explosive devices dropped harmlessly into the lake, but four bombs were heard to explode in the town and surrounds. During the weeks of rising tension and vitriolic speeches from Idi Amin, the senior staff had held meetings to plan a strategic response to any attack, so as dawn broke a medical team drove down from the hospital having realised what had happened. We found that one bomb had fallen onto the hill on which the hospital had been built, but although it had created a large crater among the loose rock it had not caused any problems with the houses on the hill. Hits were recorded in the port area, the marketplace and the fringe of the industrial area of the town. Few houses were involved so casualties were light and to our knowledge only three people died. One spectacular survivor of the raid was a tramp who regularly slept on one of the broad lower branches of a large flame tree in the marketplace. The blast of the bomb exploding 100 yards away removed him from his usual perch and in so doing blew his flimsy clothes away. He was admitted to hospital, along with other casualties from the town, moderately concussed and stark naked. As he came out of his coma after twenty-four hours he found himself the recipient of various articles of clothing donated by the surgeons looking after him, and so was perhaps the only person in Mwanza to benefit materially from the bombing raid.

The majority of the African and Asian families living in the old town sought to evacuate the women and children, along with the elderly, to the safer rural areas. The buses immediately filled up and, as every family in that part of the town had relatives living in the rural areas around Mwanza, the evacuation was both well organised and orderly. By eleven o'clock that morning we were confident that the casualties from the three main bomb sites had all been brought into the hospital so I duly set off for the Gaetje dairy to buy some fresh milk and whatever other produce they had available, anticipating that food supplies might be interrupted for a few days. Having negotiated the traffic and the queue at the dairy I came out with my purchases, only to find that a BBC news crew had arrived in a Land Rover, seemingly out of nowhere. I was pressed by the television crew to give a short interview to camera concerning the recent events in the town. I was careful to avoid giving any details about casualties, for fear of providing propaganda, but I realised that this brief interview would also assure our family and friends back at home that we were safe after the bombing raid.

Tanzania reacted to the bombing by declaring a state of emergency in Mwanza Region, with petrol rationing and a restriction on all civilian air flights. From our viewpoint on the hill high above the port we witnessed the daily build-up of tanks, jeeps and lorries arriving by rail and being transferred to the steamer for an onward journey to Bukoba and so to the Ugandan border. The appearance of the soldiers garrisoned around Mwanza also changed markedly in the short space of a week. Gone was the 'flip-flop' army in baggy Chinese fatigues, and in its place came a disciplined force in boots and smart uniforms. Small arms were issued to all soldiers and security became very tight, particularly on the hill around the hospital where a battery of anti-aircraft guns were stationed. Telephone communication was restricted to local calls only and any camera was viewed with great suspicion. These tensions were obviously being felt in the capital a thousand miles away and we suddenly became an object of concern for the British High Commission. A communication arrived from Dar es Salaam requesting the names and addresses of all British passport holders in the area. This was straightforward enough, for the two main employers in Mwanza were the hospital and the large textile mill on the outskirts of the town. There was a sizeable British population working on isolated mission stations, small farms or game reserves, and this group needed a fair amount of tracking down through contacts and friends.

John, the hospital secretary, and I collaborated on this task and eventually we sent off a fairly comprehensive list to the High Commission in Dar es Salaam. We were then informed that a Second Secretary from the High Commission would be travelling to Mwanza for a day's visit the following week, and amongst other things I was to be appointed Consul for Mwanza. This sounded very prestigious but the whole exercise that followed assumed a high degree of farce. A solemn little man arrived for this visit on one of the few civilian flights and sat down with me to agree a set of coded messages should the situation in and around Mwanza deteriorate.

'The first consignment of exercise books has arrived' would mean that things were tense and that we should stock up with flour, rice, sugar, and tinned food. I informed him that the majority of homes in this area had already carried out this precaution several weeks previously and that now none of these items were any longer available on the shops' shelves in the major stores in Mwanza.

'The second consignment of exercise books had arrived' would indicate that we should view ourselves in a war zone and we should forgather in one place and await instructions. 'Oh! So the High Commission will then make arrangements for evacuation?' I enquired.

'Well, no,' came the reply. 'That would not be possible, you see, in a war zone. But we would advise you on which route to use to leave the area.'

The gist of this message from this little diplomat was that basically we were on our own. With petrol supplies for private vehicles already scarce and the prospect of petrol rationing now looming, any question of road travel was totally irrelevant. In our position we were far more aware of the day to day variations in border tension than any office in Dar es Salaam. The Second Secretary could not wait to get back to the airport to catch his plane back to the security of the capital. He congratulated me on my appointment to Consul but then pointed out that it carried no salary, no privileges, and had no recognition from the government of Tanzania.

Several years later when I took up the appointment of Project Co-ordinator of a large British government aid programme, I found myself based at the High Commission in Dar es Salaam and so learnt first-hand of the everyday privileges of diplomatic life. Each month a consignment of foodstuffs and alcohol arrived in Dar es Salaam port, ensuring that such indispensable items as Kellogg's cornflakes, Marmite, Cooper's marmalade and cheddar cheese were always available for diplomatic families. The only complaints concerned the delay between ordering the goods and their arrival four months later. At the time of these hostilities with Uganda the food shortages in the north of Tanzania were well known in the capital. The Dutch and American embassies had made a selection of their diplomatic foodstuffs and sent crates of welcome provisions such as cheese, dried milk powder, cereals and tinned meats on to their nationals in Mwanza. But from the British High Commission we heard nothing further.

At eight o'clock on the evening of the bombing our night watchman, a veteran of the King's African Rifles in the Second World War, reported for duty and informed me that he had seen the small plane fly across Lake Victoria early the previous morning, as it had had its full identification lights on. He had watched its progress with interest and as it flew over the hill he realised that the anti-aircraft battery were all fast asleep as no shot was fired. As the aircraft turned to come in again he flung himself under our Land Rover where he heard the blast of the bomb that hit the hill. He then took me to the garage and showed me where a large piece of shrapnel had gouged out the brickwork. With great concern for our safety he suggested that we sleep away from the large glass windows and also in the lowest part of the building in case the plane should come back again.

The following day the expatriate staff of the hospital met briefly to discuss the bombing raid and plans in the event of any further attacks. We were all agreed that the most sensible and secure course of action would be to remain in Mwanza, where we not only had a job to do but we were also known and recognised. At least we had some food stocks and the hospital would receive some priority once the military authorities had built up enough food reserves for their own personnel. At this meeting the German engineer requested that we did not paint a large red cross on the roof of the hospital as he felt that such a symbol, when viewed from the air, would correspond well with the cross wires of a bomb sight on a Ugandan plane. All of us agreed with the local defence organisation's recommendation to dig slit trenches near to each house for shelter in the event of any further air raids. The hard dry soil and the considerable number of rocks and stones made this very difficult to achieve.

Other expatriate communities in the area took an entirely different view of the situation. The Italian textile workers at the local cotton mill, along with their families, pooled their petrol tokens and bought in others at exorbitant prices before heading off for Dar es Salaam in three mini buses. This proved to be a difficult journey, taking three hot days and costing them a large amount of money in unofficial petrol. They arrived in the capital in the late afternoon and drove straight to the Italian Ambassador's residence, where they found a diplomatic garden party in full swing. The Ambassador was not at all sympathetic towards their request for immediate repatriation to Italy and after a heated discussion they spent the night in a small hotel. The following day they held further discussions with the embassy staff whilst the children played on the beach, but eventually they decided that there was no alternative but to return over the 1,000 miles of rough roads back to Mwanza.

A group of Scandinavian workers with their families left Mwanza at much the same time, travelling eastwards through the great Serengeti Game Park hoping to reach the Kenyan border. During the early days of the hostilities the Tanzanian government had decided that tourism would not feature greatly in the country's immediate future and so all the lodges and hotels in the game parks were closed. Petrol supplies to the game parks were curtailed so the Scandinavians could not even refuel their vehicles and they returned even more quickly than the Italians. Understandably, the armed forces had to receive priority in the allocation of food and fuel, and so the effects of sustaining a war in an already poor country became apparent to the local population. Throughout the country the cash crops were sold on the international commodities market to raise foreign currency, so it became difficult to buy coffee, tea, rice and sugar, all of which were actually grown in Tanzania. Even maize was sold to neighbouring countries to generate some cash to support the war effort and the government encouraged every spare bit of land, every garden and field to be turned over to food-producing crops. The local nine-hole golf course in Mwanza was ploughed up and sown with maize.

Every hospital employee was encouraged to cultivate the land around their house and grow whatever crops were best suited to the conditions. Once again we set about making chicken coops in order to have a supply of fresh eggs and to this we added hutches and managed to buy a pair of mature rabbits from a local mission, as the butchery stall in the market had yet to reopen after the bombing. The flowers in the garden were replaced by maize and millet and we even planted some sugar cane in the low-lying damp area. The rabbits, as is their wont, bred very quickly and the children were delighted to be able to play with the small ones after only a few weeks. Once the litter had reached maturity I decided to despatch one or two for the freezer, as the doe was already looking pretty fecund again. I waited for the children to go to bed and then crept down the garden to select the largest of the bunch, and half an hour later it was jointed and in a polythene bag in the freezer. But I had not banked on the dedication of our nightwatchman and, a few minutes after finishing the deed, there was a loud knock on the front door. Claire and Jonathan woke up and crept out onto the landing to look through the banisters.

'Somebody has just stolen a rabbit, Doctor,' the tall ex-soldier informed me. 'When I came this evening there were seven and now there are only six in their house.'

'Oh no!' wailed Claire. 'I just hope that it's not Thumper who has been taken.'

'It might be Peter Rabbit,' piped up Jonathan. 'Can we go and look for the missing rabbit?'

'No,' I replied. 'There must be a simple explanation. Please go back to bed and I will go and have a look at the hutch with the nightwatchman.'

After this episode I took our security staff into my confidence whenever I was enhancing our meat supply.

The economic difficulties experienced by Tanzania during and after the war with Idi Amin were compounded by a steep rise in the price of oil on the world markets, and this had a knock-on effect on the price of kerosene, used in so many health centres and isolated communities for lighting, cooking and powering refrigerators. Visiting a White Father mission about an hour's drive due south from Mwanza one weekend we were amazed by the ingenuity of the two Dutch priests who had set up solar panels on the roofs of both their house and their church to provide constant running water. As this was in the heart of Sukuma country, with large herds of cattle, they also set up two methane plants on either side of the main entrance to the church. On Sunday morning the congregation arrived for church services with the women and girls carrying dustbin lids full of cow dung on their heads. They would then dutifully tip their offering into the 'open' well and leave the dustbin lid by the side to be collected after the service. The 'closed' well was sealed off to allow the methane to build up pressure, and from this gas the fathers were able to run the lights in their house and also provide a couple of gas jets on their cooking stove.

A month or so after the bombing the tense situation relaxed somewhat, as the threat of any further raids diminished following condemnation of Idi Amin by the Organisation of African Unity. Petrol restrictions were still in force, so the scope for extensive travel was restricted, but nevertheless both the local and the expatriate population were able to move around the region again with some confidence. We had received an invitation to spend a weekend with some American missionaries at a small town called Nassa, situated some forty miles from Mwanza to the south-east. The mission, along with its sizeable health centre, was run by the Maryknoll Order. This group of missionaries, founded in America at the turn of the last century, ran mission stations throughout north-east Tanzania and western Kenya. Like the White Fathers, who ran many missions to the south of Mwanza, the Maryknoll Fathers and Sisters had impeccable training in preparation for their work in Tanzania. They spoke fluent Kiswahili and were generally able to speak the tribal language (Kisukuma) as well.

The two sisters, with the assistance of well-trained Tanzanian staff, ran this large health centre in Nassa and from there had a considerable outreach programme to village dispensaries. We arrived on the Friday evening and were greeted by the two priests along with Brother John, who seemed to be a motor mechanic, carpenter, engineer and builder all in one, plus the two sisters Barbara and Catherine. The jovial, relaxed atmosphere made a pleasant change from the military presence and anti-aircraft guns around the hospital in Mwanza. The following day we joined the sisters at the health centre and it was evident that some of the small children were already showing signs of malnutrition as a result of the food shortages caused by the war effort. In conversation that evening we agreed that the situation was not severe enough to warrant food supplements at this stage, but the coming rains would have to be plentiful enough to ensure good crops in order to avoid malnutrition problems three or four months down the line.

Father Joe talked of the sudden and dramatic arrival of the rains in the previous season. Over these flat cotton-growing plains the gathering clouds and the rumble of thunder in the distant hills raised expectations and awareness, but heavy rains in these hills could result in flash flooding of the rivers and streams around Nassa within an hour or so. He recalled setting off one Sunday morning the previous year at the start of the rainy season to celebrate Mass in a mission station some fifteen miles due south of Nassa. The terrain was rough and the little church and congregation could only be reached on a small motorbike (*pikipiki* in Kiswahili). Seeing the rain clouds in the distance and hearing the rumble of thunder, Joe decided to turn his lightweight jacket around back to front to give some protection to his clerical collar and bib which he wore for the service. Sure enough, the rain started towards the end of his journey but, more importantly, the rain in the hills had swollen the rivers and streams that were flowing ever faster towards Lake Victoria. Reaching the last ford before his destination and seeing a moderate steam of water flowing across, Joe decided to have a run at it and get through on his motorbike rather than wade across the wet, sandy gully. With a good number of revs on the little bike he made it over the ford but went into a skid on the opposite bank, and he flew off his seat and over the handle bars, hitting his head on a rock and was knocked out cold. As he came round he was aware of an excruciating pain in his neck and jaw. His head was being turned through 180 degrees, as helpful hands tried to realign the face to the front of the jacket. Joe moaned an explanation that his jacket was the wrong way round and the eager parishioners on their way to the service at which he was officiating stopped trying this extreme manoeuvre and helped him towards the small chapel.

On the Sunday morning we accompanied Joe to one of the nearer mission stations which could be reached by Land Rover, and our journey was uneventful. As if conjured up by the previous day's conversation, a heavy rainstorm started halfway through the service. In Africa you can smell the rain long before you can see or feel it, and with the doors and windows of the small church wide open, the gentle breeze heralded a change in the weather. By the time the sermon came round the rain was pounding onto the corrugated iron roof with such force that none of Joe's words could be heard. With few lip readers in the congregation, Joe cut his losses and went into a lusty hymn.

On our return to Nassa we were invited to the sisters' house for lunch and there we saw Sister Catherine's prized pet – a black dachshund bitch with two puppies, who viewed our arrival with great suspicion and barking. One of the puppies was causing the sister some concern as it was a typical runt, with stunted growth, poor at feeding, and handicapped with only one eye. Catherine was debating whether to continue the struggle with this little chap or just let nature take its course. Sensing the children's concern and interest, they enquired whether we might be able to give the puppy a home and a chance to pull through. All three children were thrilled at the prospect of having a puppy so little 'Nelson' came back to Mwanza with us. With much care and attention during the weeks that followed he started to thrive and even gain weight, and by the time he was six months old Nelson had grown into a highly reliable watchdog with strength and character to match.

A few months later, as life began to return to normal after the bombing, we were able to return the hospitality of the Americans from Nassa and invited them to have an early supper with us before going out to watch a film at the local cinema in Mwanza. This cinema was a hive of activity each evening, with English films being run for three evenings of the week and Asian films for the other four. The roof was badly in need of repair and therefore during the rainy season you either had to arrive early in order to secure a seat under an intact part of the roof or you had to take a long-handled umbrella and just hope that if it did rain during the film then the run-off from the umbrella would not end up on a neighbour. There was a tacit understanding that the back five rows were kept for Tanzanians who were not fluent enough in English to follow the plot unaided; local lads fluent in English were thus able to give a simultaneous translation for the benefit of those around them.

The greatest problem of all with the cinema in Mwanza lay with the projectionist, who regularly failed to check the number of the reel that he was putting up in his attempt to ensure a smooth transition. Invariably he had reel number one in its correct place but quite often this was followed by reel three and then reel two. In the context of a thriller or a western the middle part of the film became especially confusing, with resurrections and déjà-vu effects. In spite of all the drawbacks, the Americans from Nassa thought nothing of an eighty-mile round trip to take in a movie at least once a week. A very vivid cinema experience in Mwanza was watching *The Exorcist* sat next to a seventy-year-old White Father missionary who had himself carried out several exorcisms. His whispered contributions and explanations during the course of this film made it all the more dramatic and, in the context of local superstition and witchcraft, it played to packed audiences for an extended run.

My lasting memory of the power of local superstition was walking through the market square in the midday heat at the height of the dry season. I had just looked into the covered part of the market to buy a few oranges and limes and I was on my way back home for lunch. Suddenly a hot dry wind sprang up and a dust devil came across the open part of the marketplace, sweeping up bits of cardboard, polythene wrappings and plastic cartons into a tall rotating column thirty or forty feet high. At the base of this rotating cylinder of rubbish (or *taka-taka*, as it is called in Kiswahili) the dust on the murram floor of the market was spinning around furiously. A little old Sukuma lady was walking alongside me and, seeing this phenomenon, she dropped to her knees, pulled out her rosary beads and starting praying for all she was worth that this spectre would not carry her off as well.

Two National Training Centres were located in the new hospital in Mwanza and with commendable forward planning the Ministry of Health had set them up a full year before the hospital opened. This meant that the sixth form leavers had now completed a full year of anatomy and physiology, so that as the hospital became functional they were then entering the clinical phase of their training. The nurse training school was one of three national establishments which took nurses to the equivalent of the State Registered Nurse qualification over a three-year course; one year was optional thereafter to train as a midwife. The other training school was for Medical Assistants and this was a four-year training. The first year of basic sciences was followed by three years of clinical teaching and training. Successful graduates were then posted to one of the many rural health centres or to the district hospitals where they initially worked in the daily outpatient clinics. Opportunities were available for medical assistants to continue training in the specialised fields of psychiatry, anaesthetics, and paediatrics after working for at least five years in general duties in rural areas. At a later stage it was possible for selected medical assistants to take a two-year conversion course and become fully recognised doctors.

The students' accommodation was spread over the entire top storey of the hospital so that any sound from their social life in the evenings or weekends did not disturb the patients unduly. The male students put out a very respectable football team that played against many of the local sides and always seemed to give a good account of themselves, whilst the girls teamed up with the student nurses to field two strong netball teams. The netball was fiercely competitive and I was persuaded to go down to the town and support them in a match against a local teacher training college. At half-time I wandered over to stand by the goal that our team would now be attacking and looking down I saw the head of a cockerel and two chicken's claws around the base of the goalpost.

'What on earth is that?' I asked of the nurse tutor, who was standing with me watching the game.

'Oh! That's very strong magic,' I was assured in all seriousness. 'It means that every one of our shots that hits the hoop then drops in to score.'

The students were drawn from all over Tanzania and generally were courteous, enthusiastic, and very keen to learn, which made lecturing and tutorials a real pleasure. For many of the students this was their first experience of electricity and running water, in addition to embarking on an extensive training course. One young man from Iringa in the mid-south of Tanzania confided in me upon his return from a two-week holiday at home following the successful completion of his first year, that his grandfather had found the whole concept of time very difficult to understand. Never having had a watch himself, nor a clock in his house, he argued with his grandson that there could not possibly be the same number of hours of darkness as there were of daylight. Local figures of speech in that area referred to the time of the 'little crickets' which was usually at about three o'clock in the morning, and the time of the 'large crickets' which was usually just before dawn. The concept that the hours of darkness were equal in length to the hours of daylight (when close to the equator) was something his grandfather found impossible to accept.

With the end of hostilities and the fear that they carried, the new year of 1973 brought hope, as well as a visit from the Oxfam Regional Director. Jeremy was responsible for the whole of East Africa, but Oxfam have long secured a reputation for the ability to deliver aid rapidly into those areas affected by war. With such a heavy military presence in the north-west of Tanzania, Oxfam surmised that food shortages, combined with the disruption to normal life, would probably threaten the mothers and children who are the first to suffer the effects of malnutrition and disease. Hearing of the hospital outreach programmes with their special emphasis on maternal and child health, Jeremy made contact with Elizabeth and myself. He indicated that Oxfam would be prepared to support and upgrade maternal and child health services throughout the region but they would prefer to work through the established network of government and voluntary agency maternal and child health clinics. We set up a meeting with our Regional Commissioner, a politician appointed by the President with the rank of a cabinet minister. He met up with Jeremy and ourselves and called in his Regional Medical Officer to hear what Oxfam was prepared to offer and to discuss what targets for reaching all the children under five years of age would be achievable.

With such a strong political infrastructure in place in Tanzania, much of it at that time copied from China, and with the active co-operation of the District Commissioners and the District Medical Officers, the regional maternal and child health programme was given a high profile. Education concerning the care of mothers during pregnancy and the nutrition of young children was to be strongly emphasised. New kerosene refrigerators with spare parts were to be donated to ensure the efficient storage of vaccines in the villages and small towns, many of which were far from any form of electricity supply. Oxfam also undertook to provide vaccines, especially the important and costly measles vaccine, along with their transportation from major centres to the small dispensaries and health centres. We had long suspected that many of the injections given in rural areas were ineffective, as live vaccines that had been exposed to room temperature for a few hours were rendered useless. By establishing a secure 'cold chain' from the time the vaccines were unloaded from an international flight to their storage in the kerosene refrigerator in the village, we hoped to ensure that all immunisations would be effective. Jeremy had recently been involved in the highly successful 'Blue Peter bicycles' programme that Oxfam had implemented in the area around Arusha and Moshi. He was impressed by how well the Tanzanian infrastructure had distributed these bicycles and their packs, donated by the young Blue Peter audience, to the outlying villages and dispensaries. We were delighted that the end of our first two year contract in Mwanza was being marked by such a note of optimism and valuable assistance from a well-recognised international aid organisation. We were therefore happy to indicate our willingness to the Ministry of Health to return for a further two-year contact in Mwanza.

We came back to England to find the country shivering with power cuts, a two-day working week in force in some areas, coupled with a miners' strike and all the makings of election fever as Ted Heath and Harold Wilson dominated the television screens.

## Chapter Seven

By the beginning of 1974 the tension between Uganda and Tanzania had become polarised into a state of quiet suspicion with occasional outbursts of rhetoric. Neither country could afford to sustain and equip a large army and President Nyerere was devoting his energies to improving the quality of life of the rural population of his country. Idi Amin, on the other hand, was promoting himself to lead a Pan-African army to invade Israel, an idea which he was promoting strongly after his humiliation with the raid on Entebbe Airport by the Israeli Secret Service agents. His grandiose idea found little sympathy or support amongst the other African Heads of State but nevertheless this did not prevent them from electing Amin as chairman of the Organisation of African Unity within twelve months.

In 1967 Julius Nyerere had promoted the movement of *Ujamaa* which is the Swahili for 'togetherness', and this philosophy had carried the country forward fairly well, but political awareness and enthusiasm in the villages was far behind that shown in the town areas. It was to address this imbalance that Operation Kijiji was announced in 1974, involving a rationalisation of all village life. With the realisation that it was impossible to bring the essential services of health, education, clean water and sanitation to every outlying settlement or hamlet, it was decided that all isolated settlements would be moved into established villages where the population would be large enough to support a rural health centre and a school. The first step in planning this operation was to organise a national census, and this was funded by the United Nations Organisation. So for the first time in any developing African country reliable statistics of births, deaths and population density were recorded. As all this data was being analysed the future village pattern was agreed, and arrangements were then put in hand to use the army to assist in moving subsistence farmers away from isolated settlements into established villages. The stated intention of establishing clean water and sanitation, along with schooling and health care, in the years ahead was considered justification for the obvious upheaval.

Understandably such a population movement was strongly resisted by many, particularly as the move away from a family homestead would mean leaving the graves of their ancestors and also involve a considerable journey to work their smallholding each day from wherever their new village was located. In common with many people in other parts of Tanzania, the local Sukuma opposition resorted to witchcraft in an attempt to halt the villagisation programme. Old women of evil reputation, who had traditionally been both feared and shunned, were consulted in the hope that their spells and powers would be more powerful than the army's efforts in uprooting families from their homes. The Sukuma witches either kept a hyena (in much the same way as their English equivalent used to keep a black cat) or were considered to be powerful enough to turn themselves into this creature at will. A hyena is a nocturnal animal with a powerful set of jaws, strong enough to break the thigh bone of an adult man in one crunch. The thought that these creatures would be roaming the countryside at night in search of visiting politicians or army commanders gave the local people some confidence. On the island of Ukerewe the local sorcerers, who were thought to have a special relationship with the crocodiles, arranged for many army boots to be given to the crocodiles in the hope of impeding progress. Numerous success stories abounded, but few of the illnesses or accidents that befell any of the political leaders or the army officers at that time could be attributed to attacks by wild animals or reptiles.

My first-hand experience of witchcraft at that time was both confusing and frightening. We were visiting a mission hospital with a well-run maternal and child health programme in the south of Mwanza district for the weekend, and late on the Saturday afternoon the team of nurses running their outreach clinics returned to the hospital in a state of some concern. Two nuns had been in charge of this team of three Tanzanian nurses and the clinic had been well attended. They then packed up their equipment and vaccines and prepared to leave the small township to return to the hospital some thirty miles away. The two nuns sat in the front of the Land Rover with one of the nurses while the other two nurses rode in the open part of the Land Rover pick-up with all the equipment. As the vehicle pulled away from the clinic the two young nurses in the back foolishly called out to a couple of old women selling herbal mixtures and charms that their medicine was rubbish and that this mobile team would be back in a month's time. The two old women felt both insulted and threatened by these remarks and they stood up, cursed the girls in the back of the Land Rover and ran over to throw some powder over both of them as the vehicle passed by.

By the time the Dutch doctor in charge of the hospital, with whom we had been having a quiet cup of tea, and I reached the nurses on the ward they were semi-conscious, cold, and shivering. Each had a fine rash over their arms, legs and trunk, and both had low blood pressure and a fast thready pulse. They were given steroid injections and intravenous infusions were set up. Gradually they regained consciousness over the following twenty-four hours. The nurses and all their colleagues were convinced that they had been bewitched and the sisters found it particularly difficult to staff that part of the outreach programme for several months.

With witchcraft and spells being discussed openly in public, patients started to present themselves in the hospital clinics attributing various ailments to the result of sorcery. None was more dramatic than a thirty-five-year-old man who arrived on the lake steamer from Bukoba saying that he had been suffering from a constant and painful erection for the past two days. This rare condition is called priapism, and it can be associated with blood disorders that cause clumping of the red blood cells in the erectile tissue of the penis producing a constant and painful erection. We arranged a series of blood tests but no such abnormality was demonstrated in this patient. To compound his problem the nurses on the ward seemed to show little sympathy for his condition. Local superstition dictates that this medical condition stems from having an affair with your neighbour's wife and therefore this was viewed as the price of adultery.

The Dutch surgeon and I tried a variety of procedures to reduce the erection. We injected Heparin into the erectile tissue and tried to thin the blood in order to collapse the penis. We used a strong sedative before resorting to a spinal anaesthetic, hoping to block the nervous pathways responsible for maintaining the erection. After three days the mound in the middle of the patient's bed showed no sign of lessening and the Dutch surgeon confided to me that it gave him an inferiority complex to look at it. Even Sam, the psychiatrist, was called in to try some hypnotherapy to shrink the problem, but again this was not successful. One of the Maasai male nurses told us that he had seen this condition in his homeland and he knew that there was a Maasai medicine man in the marketplace in Mwanza who might have some strong local medicine for this condition. Clutching at any straw, we encouraged him to go down to the town, and after a while he returned with a herbal mixture which had cost all of the equivalent of 5p. The patient took this mixture and his erection subsided within half an hour. In British medical textbooks such patients are said never to be able to sustain another erection and we explained this likelihood to the patient. He assured us that he had the name of the medicine man in the market from the Maasai male nurse and he was sure he could find something to restore his power, even though it might cost him a bit more than his original investment to get the erection under control.

As the villagisation process gained momentum the army started to unearth many strange medical and social problems which had been kept concealed for years. In one isolated settlement in the hills near Nassa the soldiers were in the process of helping one old woman move from her isolated home when they discovered that she was keeping a child in a cave next to the house. This 'wild child' was brought into the hospital and admitted to a single room in the psychiatric unit. It transpired that the old woman, who was known locally as a witch, had abducted the boy when he was only three years old and his parents had long given him up for dead. The old hag had kept him in a cave like an animal for the best part of four years and the sight of him was pitiful. He had long nails, dreadlocks, and a strange growth of fine hair all over his body as he moved around on all fours. He tore at any food offered to him and had no communication skills, cowering into a corner when anyone appeared. His rehabilitation took a full six months, but it was expertly organised by Sam, with the co-operation of the staff and his parents who came to live in the unit with him.

Extreme medical conditions were also brought to light by the programme which moved populations from the remote areas, and in the field of gynaecology we were confronted increasingly with the after-effects of the barbaric procedure of female circumcision. None of the Tanzanian tribes living in the north-west of the country had followed this practice in the past, but clusters of Somali had moved into the area and many of these girls had suffered as a result of either female circumcision or having their labia crudely sewn together when they were just a few months old. This latter procedure was usually carried out by a grandmother to ensure that the girl reached marriage as a virgin, but three of these young Somali girls in their late teens needed gynaecological surgery under a general anaesthetic to release these adhesions, as the crude surgery had prevented the menstrual flow from being passed.

Cases of indeterminate gender also were brought to the hospital as the subsistence farmers in these remote areas were made aware of the presence of a large hospital to serve the community. Petronella was brought into the outpatient clinic by her mother with a story that she had no vagina. Petronella seemed to be about sixteen years old and was tall and well built, with well-developed breasts. Of greater interest was the fact that Petronella had a firm swelling in each of her labia and a clitoris that was so well developed that it almost constituted a small penis. As her mother had indicated, Petronella had no vagina but her mother had hoped that a passage would develop as the girl went through puberty. As she lived so far away we admitted Petronella to hospital and sent off some urgent blood tests to Nairobi, where it was confirmed that the girl was in fact a male with XY chromosomes and the swellings in her labia were therefore testicles. This person was a victim of Testicular Feminisation Syndrome. Basically this is a defect in the metabolism of the male hormones that allows oestrogens to predominate whilst development of the baby is taking place in the uterus. Petronella had been brought up as a girl and we discussed the situation with her parents who felt that this should be the direction in which our medical assistance should go in helping her with this problem.

An operation was therefore carried out whereby the testicles were removed (the easy part) and then an artificial vagina was made for her using the lax skin from the labia to form skin flaps. These were then fixed into an artificial opening with skin grafts taken from her thighs to ensure that this channel did not close over. Petronella stayed with us in the hospital for three weeks after the operation, using a solid glass dilator to make sure that her new opening would remain open as the skin grafts gradually healed over. She realised that without ovaries and a uterus she would never be able to have children, but at least she might be able to function as a woman even though technically she was a male.

The most unfortunate girl in any community in a developing country must surely be the one who has struggled to deliver a baby whose head is too large for the mother's pelvis and so the young mother ends up with a dead baby and a hole between her bladder and her vagina through which she constantly leaks urine. Many of the Bantu women in sub-Sahara Africa encounter problems in labour in that the baby's head has a diameter which is only slightly smaller than that of the maternal pelvis. This has been attributed both to nutritional problems amongst the female population during childhood years and also to the angle at which the pelvis is set on the spine. With experience, it is possible to predict those young mothers who are probably going to encounter problems of this nature during labour. Hopefully, with improved maternity services and greater awareness in the rural populations, these young mothers can have their labour supervised in a suitable hospital where a Caesarean operation would be carried out to deliver the baby should this be necessary. Thirty years ago many of these young girls would remain in their village under the care of the traditional midwife in order to try and have their first baby at home. The labour was long and painful and the contractions of the uterus were so strong that the baby's head was pressed hard down into the base of the pelvis, trapping the bladder between the baby's head and the birth canal. The young mother would be brought into hospital but often by the time she arrived the baby had died and she would be exhausted. She would have to undergo an operation to remove the dead baby from her womb and then a few days after this operation she would start to leak urine through the hole in the bladder where the pressure of labour had shut off the blood supply and caused the tissue to die. The young girl would then become a social outcast as she was deserted by her husband, but she would also be unable to return to her parents, who probably accepted a dowry for her at her marriage ceremony.

The surgical repair of these so-called vesico-vaginal fistulae was not followed by any reasonable success rate until a husband and wife team devoted a lifetime's work to treating groups of patients at their hospital in Ethiopia. The Hamlyns (both doctors from Australia) found this problem to be so common in their part of Ethiopia that they formed a village around their hospital where the sufferers lived before and after surgery. In this way the poor smelly outcasts who arrived could understand that not only was their condition shared by others but it could be cured. Several of the Hamlyns' patients stayed on at the hospital following successful surgery and were subsequently trained as nurses and theatre assistants, giving even greater educational emphasis to the programme. Indeed one of their trained surgeons there started by assisting at fistula repair operations and later became the surgeon in charge of the unit as the Hamlyns went into retirement. This husband and wife team achieved an 80% success rate in closing these defects and restoring the young girls to a normal life, and more importantly to social acceptability.

I was fortunate enough to meet up with Ted Hamlyn at a meeting of surgeons in Nairobi and was present when he demonstrated the surgical techniques of his procedure. Naturally, we attempted to establish facilities at the regional hospital in Mwanza, and although we could not provide the huge social and emotional support before and after the operation that Ted and his wife were able to offer to Ethiopia, nevertheless our success rate improved considerably and we achieved closure of these debilitating fistulae in 60% of our patients.

In common with many other African countries Tanzania suffered problems with venereal disease at that time, and for the young women in particular gonorrhoea was a real problem. This disease produces few if any symptoms in the woman until she becomes aware that she is infertile. The chronic infection and pus act to block her tubes that carry the egg from the ovary into the uterus and thus a large proportion of our young gynaecological patients in Mwanza were women with blocked tubes and chronic abscess cavities in their lower abdomen. Surgery was carried out to attempt to clear the infection and to re-establish the patency of the tubes, but few of these operations resulted in successful pregnancies. There was a high risk of an ectopic pregnancy (where the gestational sac develops outside the uterus, either in the tube or close to the ovary) and this often ruptures in the early weeks of pregnancy, with dramatic internal bleeding.

One of our patients did become pregnant and the sac developed in the abdominal cavity, with the placenta (behaving like a large parasite) taking its blood supply from the bowel wall, the bladder and other organs. Fortunately, we realised the situation halfway through the pregnancy and we were able to persuade the mother to move very close to the hospital. Some three weeks before the due date we carried out a complicated procedure, in conjunction with the general surgeons, to deliver a live baby and we made no attempt to remove those parts of the placenta which had become adherent to vital structures.

Such was the depth of gratitude amongst these patients that many mothers chose to name their baby after the obstetrician following a traumatic delivery which resulted in a live birth. I subsequently came across children out in the bush clinics who were called Evansi. But I have to admit that there were also children who were called Datsun, Toyota and Peugeot after the particular vehicles in which their mothers were travelling had failed to reach the hospital on time.

Within the first few months of our time in Mwanza I had to go to Nairobi to attend a meeting of surgeons, and was fortunate to get a lift there and back in the Land Rover of Klaus, the son of Mrs Gaetje who ran the farm across the water. Klaus was an expert mechanic and therefore it was doubly comforting not only to be driven by him but also to be assured that he could cope with any problem that might beset the vehicle during the journeys. Whilst in Nairobi I was able to acquire a very good second-hand safari tent, which was designed to sleep six adults and also had a veranda enclosed by strong mosquito netting. We were thus able to spend long weekends and holidays visiting the various attractions in northern Tanzania without having to worry about the cost of accommodation.

At that time there were often recognised camping sites close to the game park lodges, for which the authorities made only a nominal charge provided that we booked the services of a game park guide and took dinner in the lodge. With the western gate of the famous Serengeti Game Park ('Serengeti' in the Maasai language means 'extended place') just ninety minutes' drive from Mwanza, we had several trips exploring this famous park at different times of the year. Again the contrast with Uganda was obvious, as the size of this game park (13,000 square kilometres) covers the same area as Northern Ireland. Each year towards the end of May the grazing on the main Serengeti plains becomes exhausted and so a huge migration, mainly of wildebeest and Burchell's zebra, takes place. A long column of these animals, often several miles long, starts to move west before then turning north in order to find fresh grazing. With approximately one million wildebeest the migration is followed by sundry predators (lion, leopard, cheetah and hyena) all anxious to pick off the slower, weaker animals of the migrating herds.

Fort Ikoma was the nearest game park lodge to Mwanza and, being situated in the north-west part of the Serengeti, it benefited from seeing the migration once a year. This old fort with its castellated walls was built at the turn of the last century and fell to British forces towards the end of the First World War in 1917. It lay as a ruin until after the Second World War when its tourist potential was realised and the thick walls of the old building were opened up and converted into the public rooms of a game lodge. A tented camp was erected next door to the fort buildings but still within the compound of the old fort itself. Naturally, a military construction of this type occupied one of the highest hills for miles around and so superb views of the Serengeti stretched as far as the eye could see from almost every aspect of the fort. Inez and Skip, the Anglo-American owners of the tourist lodge, were kind enough to permit us to pitch our tent at the end of their tented accommodation. They allowed us to use the dining room in the lodge in the evening as well as the swimming pool in the afternoon after a day of viewing the animals.

On one of our first visits to Fort Ikoma a large party of Americans was occupying the tented village, and after dinner in the evening they eventually retired to their camp beds and canvas cover. One of the party was a fairly good mimic of many of the animals that he had seen that day and from the privacy of his tent he regaled his fellow tourists with his imitations of elephant, buffalo, jackal, and others. The audience was greatly appreciative but, as our tent was next door to this natural mimic, we realised that he had fallen asleep well before his fellow tourists. At that same moment a couple of hyenas started to walk around the tented village making their characteristic laughing howl.

'Oh, that was great, Arine! Do it again.'

The hyenas duly obliged. Peals of laughter rang out from the other tents.

'Do it again. Do it again, Arine, that was really great.'

Eventually the hyenas decided that the tourists were making so much noise that they sloped off into the night in search of a quieter location. At breakfast the following morning Arine was congratulated by many of his compatriots on his skill, especially the hyena. A slightly puzzled look crossed his face.

During our time in Mwanza we were privileged to entertain a number of medical students who had contacted either the hospital or myself directly to spend their elective period gaining some experience of medicine in a developing country. As the children were fairly young it was possible for them to squeeze into one end of the tent and so allow space for a medical student to come on these safaris with us. Medical students were usually encouraged by their teaching hospitals to spend up to three months of the first part of their final year on any attachment in general practice or overseas medicine that would give them a wider perspective when they qualified as doctors. Our first elective student was Paul, who not only played the guitar very well but also had a good singing voice and a wide repertoire of songs which ranged from English folk songs to *Peter, Paul and Mary*, all of which the children picked up very quickly. Tim joined us a few months after Paul had left and was also a senior student at my old teaching hospital, King's College Hospital in south London.

Tim was very laid back and managed to learn several significant phrases in Kiswahili which he used to good effect when he joined me in the gynaecology clinics. He chose to travel back home to England via Nairobi and to this end he left Mwanza by bus and found himself to be the only European on the coach when they came to the Tanzanian/Kenyan border. The customs officer seemed to show a somewhat prejudiced interest in Tim's rucksack and questioned him in Kiswahili. Tim could not understand what the officer was concerned about as the man spoke no English. Tim's Swahili was very limited and in desperation he came out with his stock phrase:

'Please take your pants off. Lie up on the bed and let your knees fall apart while I examine you.'

His fellow passengers cracked up with laughter; the customs officer was acutely embarrassed and waved him straight through and on his way to Nairobi.

Jean and Malcolm joined us from the London Hospital; they were newlyweds and seemed to be on some sort of perverse honeymoon in Tanzania. As Jean was a laboratory technician, she and Malcolm stayed with Barbara and John and joined us for one of our safaris in the Serengeti. They were fiendishly good at Scrabble which we seemed to play until very late at night by the light of a gas-powered hurricane lamp.

John and David then joined us from St Mary's Hospital, but

they only stayed for six weeks as they were anxious to return for the start of the rugby session, both coming from South Wales. They pursued their fitness regime with evening training runs once the sun had lost its fierce heat. This caused some concern to the anti-aircraft battery stationed on the hill near the hospital, and we had to calm things down with the local artillery commander, explaining that the training regime was not military spying but aimed at football prowess.

Karen was a Cambridge graduate, and she had the most unpleasant introduction to an elective period in Africa. On her very first evening with us I was called out around dusk to see a young woman who had been admitted in a state of severe shock with a presumed ectopic pregnancy. I went into the hospital and this was indeed the situation that faced us. Thinking that Karen would be interested in seeing the operation, I telephoned home and suggested that she came into the hospital through the main gate and asked to be directed to the operating theatres. She presented herself at the main gate of the hospital in the clothes that she had worn to travel out from England, and this comprised a sleeveless top and a rather short miniskirt, which was fashionable at the time. The militia man in his grey fatigues on duty at the hospital gate took exception to this dress code and immediately arrested her. Naturally, Karen could not understand a word of what was being said or even appreciate the problem that had caused her to be detained.

A Tanzanian nurse arriving for night duty had assessed the situation and felt rather sorry for the young English girl, so came down to the operating theatres to tell me what had occurred. I left the theatre and went up to the front gate and explained to the man that as this young lady had just arrived from England, she was obviously not aware of the local dress code, and that once he had released her then she would ensure that she dressed herself more appropriately in the future. None of this cut any ice; he was reluctant to accept my reassurance and stood on his dignity. I took Karen by the arm and gently pushed the man to one side to allow Karen to come into the hospital. Unfortunately he caught his heel on an uneven paving slab and fell backwards into a prickly pear cactus. I hurried into the hospital with Karen and found the rear entrance. I suggested that she went straight back to our house and had a stiff drink to get over this experience. I then returned to the theatre and undertook the operation to remove the ectopic pregnancy and also auto-transfuse a considerable amount of blood loss.

As I came out of the operating theatre I was confronted by three soldiers with sub-machine guns who arrested me for assaulting one of the People's Militia. I was driven down to the police station in the back of a Land Rover under armed guard and handed over to the police authorities. Fortunately, the Superintendent of Police, who was on duty that evening and who was summoned in from his home to take a statement from me, was fairly well known to the obstetric department. His wife was expecting her first baby and it was a twin pregnancy. She had experienced several complications and had been admitted to hospital two or three times and so I knew the couple very well. He was sympathetic and listened to my side of the story before waiting for all the military vehicles to leave the police station compound. He then organised one of his police Land Rovers to take me back home, and for the remainder of the ten weeks Karen kept her legs reasonably well covered whenever we were in the hospital or the town. Clearly the experience did not have any lasting effect on Karen, as she went on to become a consultant gynaecologist and obstetrician herself.

We were able to use our large safari tent to camp on the rim of the Ngorongoro Crater at a campsite there with a truly spectacular view over this wonder of the natural world. The crater is the largest unbroken caldera in the world, and access down the 610 metre descent to the crater floor is made by a rough winding track, suitable only for four-wheel-drive vehicles. We were able to take some of our elective students on these weekend trips to give them a flavour of wildlife safaris, especially as the crater floor guaranteed seeing rhino, lion and leopard and, if the soda lake had water, then the flamingos set off the whole experience. Occasionally the young Maasai morani warriors would wander through the campsite in the evening with their elaborate hairstyles and long spears. As usual they were fascinated by the straight blond hair of Claire and Jonathan and mildly curious about the sort of food we were cooking in the evening. Stopping on our way back to Mwanza after one such camping trip for lunch at Seronera Lodge, the headquarters of the Serengeti, we met up with a party of tourists who had just flown into the Serengeti from Arusha. Over drinks before lunch I enquired of one of the party what their plans were for the following day.

'Oh I'm not sure where we are right now, but I'm told that in the morning we're driving out of here to visit Nicaragua and look at that volcano.'

The last medical student to seek an attachment came all the way from California. He was a delightful extrovert who evoked incredible curiosity amongst the nurses by changing the colour of his contact lenses each day of the week. Doctors are trained to be observant but I had failed to notice that Hunt appeared on the wards with a hazel pair of contact lenses on Monday, a light grey pair on Tuesday, a blue pair on Wednesday, and by then the nurses were beside themselves with curiosity. Without exception these students were all delightful house guests, highly motivated in their quest for knowledge, and totally immersed in the short-term tasks of their elective period. Hunt has recently retired from medicine in California and he and his wife have recently both learnt Spanish and they have now gone to work in Guatemala in one of the more remote mountainous areas.

The year 1974 saw great changes in the staffing structure of the hospital in Mwanza. In the two key posts senior Tanzanian staff arrived to replace the American medical superintendent and the Dutch matron and both of these proved to be very good key appointments. A well-qualified and highly motivated paediatrician then arrived, having completed postgraduate studies at Great Ormond Street Hospital in London. Valerian not only worked tirelessly, often in the premature baby unit, but also proved to be an excellent administrator. Many of the original expatriate staff whose salaries were 'topped up' by Miserior finished their contract and left, to be replaced by specialists from Hungary and India. In addition, a Russian medical team arrived with specialists in eyes, general surgery, anaesthetics, and general medicine from the medical school in Novosibirsk in Siberia. In some of our neighbouring regions Chinese medical teams were posted to work in one or two of the district hospitals, and during one of our outreach programmes I had the privilege to watch a Chinese medical team carry out major abdominal surgery without conventional anaesthesia and using only acupuncture. At that time the Chinese government was undertaking a major engineering programme in Tanzania to provide a new railway connection from Dar es Salaam to the border with Zambia in the far south west. The then government in South Africa had closed its ports to Zambian exports of copper and the Chinese were jointly engaged by the Zambian and Tanzanian governments to run the new railway line, allowing Zambia access to Tanzania's port on the Indian Ocean. Many Chinese medical teams accompanied this project, but those that were surplus to requirements in the southern part of the country were posted to work in hospitals in other regions of Tanzania. From my limited experience of their work over that one day it did seem that they provided a welcome and effective service, but there was an obvious lack of communication. With the great differences between Chinese traditional medicine and the Western pattern (which had been established in Tanzania for so long) there was no possibility of training local staff to continue the work that the Chinese had started.

In 1975 a Tanzanian obstetrician and gynaecologist was appointed to Mwanza, and this was a real red-letter day for both our department and the hospital. My Hungarian colleague had been brought out of retirement to come to work in East Africa and was a delightful, cultured person with a good command of English and professionally very competent. Although he enjoyed the chance to live outside a communist country for a couple of years both he and his wife looked forward to the day when they could return home to their beloved Budapest. The arrival of Ambrose from his postgraduate training in Leeds was most welcome for all of us in the department. Ambrose's family home was just eighty miles south of Mwanza and by tribe he was a Sukuma. During his first month he swears that he saw almost every female member of his extended family in his gynaecology clinic, but after that the pressure eased considerably and he was able to take over the administration and running of the department.

Towards the end of 1975, Jeremy, the Oxfam Regional Director, returned to Mwanza to assess the benefits of the maternal and child health programme which they had been funding for our region. We were delighted to report that the teams in the region had hit an 80% target of immunisation of the under-five population, and that 90% of the pregnant mothers in the region had received antenatal care. The experiment of allowing the mothers to keep their own antenatal cards had worked well, as they could attend either a dispensary, a health centre or a hospital and still maintain continuity of antenatal care. The kerosene refrigerators in the dispensaries and health centres had been well maintained and the 'cold chain' for the vaccines had been unbroken from the airport right to the small dispensaries. These live vaccines were often administered under the shade of a mango tree, as the numbers of mothers and small children made it impossible to cram everybody inside the small buildings. As a result of the great support received from Oxfam the Regional Commissioner invited me to attend the annual regional development meeting some three weeks later and to address the delegates on the successes that had been achieved. At the same time I was to introduce the senior Tanzanian nurse who was going to take over the administration of the programme and so use some leverage on the delegates to negotiate a realistic budget for the following year.

With some trepidation I addressed the delegates in my best Kiswahili and managed to get the historical background along with the aims and objectives across to the audience fairly effectively. At the close of that particular section the Regional Commissioner indicated that he had received a message of commendation from the Minister of Health in Dar es Salaam and asked the clerk to hand it to me so I could read it to the assembled delegates. I had to explain:

'I am very sorry to say that I have learnt all my Kiswahili by ear, mainly in the course of conversation, so that with regard to reading and writing your language I fear I am totally illiterate.'

'In that case,' replied the Regional Commissioner, smiling broadly, 'perhaps you ought to stay on for the next section concerning adult literacy, which is a project that has been sponsored by UNICEF, and we can then put you in touch with your nearest adult literacy centre.'

We had regretfully decided that, as we neared the end of our second two-year tour of duty in Tanzania, Elizabeth needed to attain some specialist qualifications in maternal and child health education. Claire and Jonathan had reached the upper classes of the little English primary school in Mwanza and so we would all have to consider a change in direction after I had completed my second contract in May 1976.

Such a decision always causes rifts and separations, and none more so than with our excellent house girl, Sisilia, who had looked after us as a family so well during our time in Mwanza. We did eventually find her employment with great friends, who also had a young family and who would appreciate Sisilia's qualities in childcare, cooking and housework, for which she had no equal. The other area of anxiety concerned the dogs. Sally, our acquisition from Uganda, had long since deserted us for the company of our neighbours two doors away, who had three very young children yet to start school and were around the home every hour of the day often with food and tempting titbits readily available.

Nelson, our one-eyed dachshund, whom we had obtained from the sisters at Nassa, was among our prime concerns. One of the senior diplomats at the British High Commission in Dar es Salaam, with whom I had stayed whilst I was lecturing at the University Medical School, was most anxious to adopt our little dog. He even agreed to continue with the strange dietary pattern that had evolved over the years.

In the early days Nelson was fed on fresh heart from the local butcher, as there seemed to be little demand for this type of offal from the local people, and Nelson devoured it eagerly. We did notice that feeding time outside the back door was always accompanied by a cacophony of barking and on investigating this further we found that the kites circling overhead had also developed a taste for the chunks of heart. These huge birds would come swooping down every afternoon at feeding time to carry off Nelson's bits and pieces of food in their talons. By freezing the heart and then cutting it into deep frozen chunks we managed to break this pattern as the birds were unable to cope with the frozen meat. Nelson continued to devour his meal with great relish and without interference. He then returned indoors, only to sit and shiver for half an hour whilst his stomach warmed up the load.

Nelson took a tearful farewell of all the family the week before we were due to depart, as I had arranged to take him with me on my last trip to Dar es Salaam by air. All expatriates had to satisfy the income tax department in person that they were up to date with their tax affairs and then obtain the necessary stamp on their passport to allow them to leave the country. I booked my ticket and confirmed that I could take a small dog instead of hand luggage. Elizabeth drove me to the airport with the children and there were tearful farewells whilst I went up to the check-in.

'Good morning. I am booked on this morning's flight to Dar. My name is Doctor Evans, and I am accompanied by this small dog.'

'Your ticket is confirmed. Have you the necessary veterinary certificate for the dog and the cage for his transportation?'

'Your office in the town told me I could just take the dog on board on the lead.'

'That is not possible, sir. If you wish to take the dog you will have to observe the regulations and produce a veterinary cheti.'

We returned to the car and I rummaged through my medicine bag for a suitable tranquiliser. I slipped it to Nelson and waited ten minutes for him to feel a bit drowsy before wrapping him in a small cotton cloth and placing the entire bundle into a local woven basket. I then said goodbye to the family again and found a different clerk at the check-in desk.

'Oh good morning, sir. Do you have any luggage?'

'Good morning. Yes, I have just hand luggage thank you, my briefcase and a basket of pineapples which I will keep with me on board.'

I was allocated a window seat, and as the other passengers boarded I was dismayed to see that a Tanzanian lady of more than generous proportions was making for the empty aisle seat next to mine. As the Fokker Friendship plane warmed up its engines before take-off I leant down and stroked Nelson, by way of a comforting gesture. My neighbour looked at me quizzically.

'Pineapples,' I explained. 'For our friends in Dar.'

The whole flight proceeded very well but by the time we were making our approach to Dar es Salaam airport the effect of the tablet was wearing off quite quickly and the basket was making large involuntary movements around my feet. The lady next to me was obviously very apprehensive about flying, as she had consumed several large bottles of beer during the flight. My hand luggage coming to life near her feet made her eyes stand out like organ stops but she obviously put the experience down to the alcohol she had consumed, groaned quietly and closed her eyes ready for landing.

Nelson quickly settled into his new surroundings during the three days that I spent in Dar es Salaam and from then on enjoyed a privileged life as a diplomatic dog.

A few days later we had no similar problems in getting the children on board an identical aircraft at Mwanza which flew us to Nairobi, where we linked up with the British Airways flight to London. We returned to the long hot summer of 1976 and all the fascination of the Olympic Games on television.

# Chapter Eight

'Hello. Is that Doctor Evans speaking?'
'Yes. This is Richard Evans.'
'Well good morning, Doctor Evans. This is Sister Barbara here from Waterford in Ireland. Now you don't know me but I am the Matron of Airmount Hospital in Waterford, which is run by the Medical Missionaries of Mary. You worked with our sisters in Uganda five years ago and it is through them that I have found your address and telephone number.'
'Well, yes; it's very nice to speak with you, Sister.'
'Now. I wonder if you can help us. You see, our senior consultant obstetrician here has just run off with his secretary to Canada and he has left a distraught wife and five children behind in Waterford. Now, we cannot expect you to help out with that situation but we do need somebody to cover his work over here and we wonder whether you would consider coming to work a six-month locum for us?'

At the time that this conversation took place in July we were staying with my mother in the large family home in Nottingham. The early summer months had drifted by with plans changing by the day. Elizabeth wanted to do a master's degree in maternal and child health and had considered Nottingham University as a possibility, but eventually found the course and the entry requirements at Dundee were more suited to her needs. I had taken a short-term senior registrar locum in obstetrics and gynaecology at the professorial unit at the new medical school of Nottingham University. After working there for two weeks the professor was kind enough to call me into his office and encourage me to apply for the definitive position of senior registrar, which would run for the next four years and this would eventually lead on to a consultant appointment. I was already aware, however, that my work in East Africa over the last seven years had taken me far down the route of obstetrics and gynaecology in a developing country. Perhaps the experience and skills that I possessed were not well suited to the academic life in a teaching hospital in the Midlands.

This offer from Ireland came as a pleasant surprise and afforded a totally new direction to any plans that we were formulating. At the very least it would offer six months of relative stability in a rented, unfurnished house and a chance to unpack all our luggage, which had arrived by sea and was currently being stored in the garage of my mother's home. With such pleasant memories of working with these nuns in Uganda, I decided to fly over to Ireland and meet the small community of sisters in Waterford. In addition I would be interviewed by the hospital secretary of Ardkeen Hospital in the town, as part of my duties would involve gynaecology at this government hospital under the control of the South East Health Board.

A few days later I boarded an early morning flight from East Midlands Airport, and we were soon flying over the parched brown fields of middle England which, in the severe drought conditions of 1976, were more reminiscent of the East African savannah. Once across the Irish Sea the fields were really green, so the Emerald Isle really did exist after all. The rail journey to Waterford, on a single track line, was speedy enough and I was met by Sister Barbara, who drove me to Airmount Hospital, on a hill above Waterford. Here I met the other four sisters working in the hospital complex there. Following an early lunch I was then driven to Ardkeen Hospital in the town where a short interview was conducted. At the end of the day I was then offered the position of locum consultant for a six-month period, to start as soon as was possible.

Upon returning to Nottingham we discussed the move to Waterford and it seemed to be acceptable to all parties involved, so Elizabeth made arrangements to start the course at Dundee University in September. It took us only a few days to pack up the bits and pieces of our belongings and organise a container to take these, plus all the crates of sea freight, to Fishguard and so on to Waterford. We ourselves followed the same route by car a few days later and so I was ready to start work by late July.

The day after we arrived in Ireland to start this assignment the British Ambassador to Ireland, Christopher Ewart-Biggs, was murdered by the IRA. A landmine blew up the armour-plated car in which he and his private secretary were travelling, just yards from the gates of his official residence in south Dublin.

Without much of a head for business, I had assumed that the sisters at Ardkeen Hospital offered a combined service in obstetrics and gynaecology that would generate a salary cheque in my direction at the end of each month. I was soon informed by the South East Health Board that such a cheque would be issued, but only for the services which I had given to those patients who were entitled to free healthcare. At that time in Ireland this patient category accounted for only 30% of the population. These were the unemployed, those on low income, and families farming less than forty acres. So in addition to what I considered a very reasonable salary for working five half days per week, I also found myself responsible for a large number of private patients who were not covered by health insurance. This was to form the bulk of the work at Airmount Maternity Hospital.

Up to this time I had never indulged in the experience of private practice, and in Tanzania it was government policy not to allow any member of the medical staff employed by the Ministry of Health to take any form of payment from patients. The difference in the pattern of work became evident within my very first week, as my antenatal clinic at Airmount seemed to be going very slowly. In spite of the full waiting room there seemed to be a great delay between patients.

'Things seem to be running very slowly this afternoon, Sister.'

'Yes, Doctor. You see, there is a problem because of the bank strike.'

Now I was well aware that all the high street banks in Ireland were on strike at that time, but I failed to see how this could influence the running of my clinic and I informed sister accordingly.

'Ah that's where you are wrong now, Doctor. You would not want to be accepting cheques from patients that you cannot cash for months now, would you?' she informed me. 'So your secretary out there is insisting on cash for all your consultations and that means that some of the patients, or their husbands, have to go off and get the cash before we'll let them in to see you.'

Sure enough at the end of this clinic I was presented with a large packet containing a variety of banknotes, English, Irish and even samples from some of the Scottish banks.

I also had a great problem with Wednesdays during those early weeks. I could find nothing in my timetable, either at Airmount or Ardkeen, for that day of the week and I was anxious in case I was expected at a clinic in an outlying hospital. I approached Sister Barbara on the subject.

'I seem to have nothing to do on Wednesdays, Sister. What was the previous timetable, and where should I be working this day of the week?'

'Well now, during the winter he was away hunting every Wednesday and then in the summer wasn't he away fishing most Wednesdays.'

'And during the spring and the autumn?' I queried.

'Well now,' Sister Barbara quipped, 'perhaps that was when he was with his secretary.'

I accepted the fact that every Wednesday was a day off.

Our rented house was on a new housing estate just outside Waterford and close to Ardkeen Hospital. It was very comfortable and practical, with a small garden running down to open fields. We were fortunate to have friendly neighbours, most of whom had young children who were quick and ready to befriend our gang. Schooling for the children was sorted out and Claire, being ten years of age, would be studying both Gaelic and Irish country dancing. Even with the emphasis on Gaelic in schools I was impressed by the correctness of the English spoken in Ireland. Their pronunciation stressed the 'c' in appreciation or the well-sounded 'm' in film. Whilst this may be deemed quaint, the sentence construction and the correct use of adverbs and adjectives was universally observed. Nowadays we seem to accept the lazy patterns of speech 'he played solid' or 'I don't feel good' that would evoke peals of laughter in Ireland.

Having said this I recall my first weekend on call a few days after arriving in Waterford. Just as I was going to bed, soon after ten o'clock, the phone rang and I picked it up.

'Hello, Doctor Evans speaking.'

'Goodnight Doctor,' said a pleasant female voice.

'Goodnight,' I replied and replaced the receiver, thinking that some efficient member of staff was checking my phone and my availability. But the phone soon rang again and I answered it promptly.

'Goodnight Doctor Evans, and please don't hang up on me. This is the duty midwife here and we would like you to come to the labour ward, please.'

I then learnt that 'goodnight' in Ireland is a greeting used after darkness and does not have the finality with which it is associated in England.

The first two weeks in Waterford were difficult, not because the work was taxing or stressful; compared with the nine thousand deliveries a year in Mwanza the obstetric workload in Airmount was very manageable. The real problem arose with the dockyard security forces in Fishguard impounding all containers destined for Ireland in an enhanced security exercise following the assassination of the British Ambassador. The sisters at Airmount were kind enough to lend us basic cooking utensils and crockery, and so we spent our first two weeks in Waterford camping out in a rented house. We had managed to bring over a number of pictures and artefacts in the back of the car, and as we had no luggage to unpack I set off into the town in search of some tools, screws and hooks to fix these items around the house and make it seem less austere. I was recommended to try The Quay in Waterford, where I found an old-fashioned hardware store with wooden boards on the floor and a counter running the length of the shop. High shelves went up the back wall almost to ceiling height and there seemed to be a strong smell of putty and sandpaper. An elderly man wearing brown overalls finished his conversation with a group of local handymen and turned to me.

'Good morning, sir, what can I do for you?'

'I'd like a medium-sized claw hammer, please.'

'Just behind you, sir,' he said, pointing over my shoulder at the shelf. 'You can take your pick from the three sizes there.'

I selected the hammer of my choice.

'I'd also like some three-quarter-inch tacks and some picture hooks, please.'

'Now for those you go along the counter, that's it. Now turn right and they are on the fourth shelf up.'

I helped myself to a packet as directed. And so it was that I continued to help myself to the various items I needed but I now found myself at the far end of the counter close to the exit of the shop onto a parallel road. As I had all my purchases in my hand I thought it best to settle up with the assistant at this end of the store and so avoid running the gauntlet of the audience stretched out along the counter.

'Can I settle up here, please? How much do I owe you?'

'I'll put it on your account,' called out my friendly assistant down the length of the counter.

'But I haven't got an account!'

'You have now, sir.'

'But you don't know who I am!'

'I'll find out. Don't worry. Goodbye now.'

The container arrived a few days later and was unpacked with great gusto. The house suddenly became furnished and full of long-lost toys and Lego sets, whilst books were restored to grateful owners. But by the time mid-August had arrived the hot weather to which we had returned some three months earlier had given way to cold winds and driving rain, and in spite of turning the heating up in the house we were all feeling the cold. I set out again for the friendly hardware store where I had an account. Many people seemed to be taking refugee in this store from the horizontal rain that was lashing across The Quay in Waterford. I found my friendly man in his brown overalls and made an enquiry.

'Could I have four hot-water bottles, please?'

At this request the whole store fell silent. Many of the customers had come in with the intention of making a purchase but stopped in their tracks when hearing my question. My creditor, now aware that he had the full attention of everyone in the store replied to me.

'Are you aware, sir, that we are in the height of summer and that all the factories are closed this week for their summer holidays?'

I tried to make some excuse about being unduly sensitive to this cold August weather and he smiled.

'The hot-water bottles are upstairs amongst the winter stock. I'll bring some down for you now but don't go persuading these people that the summer is over.'

When we were packing up the house in Mwanza, and collecting all the items that we intended to take back to Europe with us, a Sikh friend, whose father owned a timber business, suggested that we constructed crates from planks of well-seasoned local African hardwood. When dismantled this could then be used to make attractive and durable furniture. This seemed a good idea at the time, and now with the unpacking complete I surveyed a stack of heavy, slightly rough boards. I put the word out among my neighbours for a good local carpenter who could fashion a refectory table and two benches out of this timber. A recommendation duly came through and I visited this man at his house where he had his own small workshop. I took him out and showed him the planks in the back of the estate car.

'I have obviously never worked with this sort of wood before, but I'll be delighted to give it a try. However, these planks will need to be planed before I can start to use them for furniture. You'll need an industrial plane to do that.'

'Well, who in Waterford has an industrial plane that we can use?'

'You could try Phelan's Undertakers, they have an industrial plane and they would plane these planks down for you, I'm sure. They put through batches of elm planks once a week and they would do this for you with no trouble.'

So the following Wednesday I loaded the rough hardwood

boards into the back of the Volvo estate and drove them over to the undertakers, wondering whether all this trouble was worth a few sticks of furniture. Phelan's were very cooperative when I introduced myself and outlined the problem. They agreed to do the work for a very small charge, and the following Wednesday I collected the transformed planks. Already the grain of the wood could be seen, along with the deep natural colour of the hardwood.

The next morning I was halfway through a hysterectomy on my operating list when the theatre nurse on the trolley said to me in a low voice:

'I hear you have already visited the local undertaker and made yourself known to him.'

'How did you know that?' I asked.

'Oh, in this town there is a very good information service. Mind you, I was surprised that you found it necessary to spend an hour there since in this speciality we shouldn't lose too many, should we?'

I started to explain about the timber, but her eyes, which were the only part of her I could see with the theatre mask in place, glazed over and I knew that she was sticking with her version of events. Nevertheless two weeks later I took delivery of a beautiful table with two bench seats and well worth all the scandal of a new doctor who had gone out of his way to make friends with the undertaker.

By the time early September had arrived Elizabeth had left for Dundee to commence her course and the children had started at their local schools. Claire found that both Gaelic language and Irish dancing were in her syllabus but she was not too daunted and found both enjoyable. Jonathan never had an easy relationship with maths in those days and the first homework that he brought home during his first week was refreshingly practical: 'If I put five shillings each way on a horse at four to one and it comes in second, how much do I win?'

Jonathan quickly developed a love affair with hurling, a sport played with a hardball and what looks like an oversized hockey stick. As the two sons of one of our neighbours were keen players we were forced to go on the hunt for two hurleys, the stick being carved out of a single piece of elm. The rules of the game are fairly broad, as the ball can touch most parts of the body without a foul being incurred. The basic skill lies in flicking the ball off the ground with the hurley and then, whilst it floats in mid-air, a full swing of the stick is used to propel the ball forward at great speed and often a huge distance. Jim, who was my house surgeon at Ardkeen for those few months, was a county hurling player and managed to get every Saturday afternoon off during the winter months to play. Jim, in common with many other good hurling players, had several old fractures of his nose and a partial upper denture to testify to his skill at the game.

The autumn in Waterford passed happily enough for the children and myself. The work was busy during the day, and as a rule I managed to organise my timetable to be home in the late afternoon when the schools finished. The sisters approached me to see if I would consider applying for the permanent position of consultant obstetrician and gynaecologist as this post was due to be advertised in early November. After some discussion within the family I went ahead and submitted an application when the advertisement duly appeared.

A few weeks later I was on the train to Dublin for an interview for the post. The interview panel was composed of two consultants in obstetrics and gynaecology and two hospital administrators. When the interview started there seemed to be some sympathy for my recent background in East Africa, viewing it as interesting but not necessarily relevant to the needs of Waterford. A few concerns were expressed about my experience in operative obstetrics and gynaecological surgery. After half an hour we shook hands and I was then informed that the second part of the interview process would now take place in a small room down the corridor. This came as a complete surprise and I had no idea what lay ahead.

I was ushered into a small room and presented with two papers to translate; one was English to Irish and the second Irish to English. I politely explained to the secretary of the interviewing board that I had no ability whatsoever in the Gaelic language and, although I was fluent in Kiswahili, I was unable to even translate the English into that language being only slightly literate. The sisters were kind enough to explain to me later that as the greater part of the post was funded by the South East Health Board, this was probably viewed as a civil service interview for which a working knowledge of the Irish language was obligatory.

I left the interview halls in a bit of a daze, not relishing the prospect of packing everything up again and leaving Waterford in midwinter after just one term in the new schools for the children. I rapidly lost my sense of direction in Dublin and soon had no idea how to find the station. I asked a passer-by for help.

'Excuse me. Could you tell me the way to the railway station, please?'

'Well now. If I were going there I really wouldn't start from here.'

But all the same he did manage to give me some fairly sensible directions and I linked up with my train in fairly good time. As the train rattled through the grey light of the November evening I flicked through the pages of the *British Medical Journal* that I had tucked into my briefcase and ended up in the back pages where all the oversees posts were advertised.

A large box advert caught my eye detailing the position of general surgeon, with experience in obstetrics and gynaecology, to a group of islands in the Pacific Ocean. The post was being advertised by the Overseas Development Ministry in London and carried an addendum: 'French speaking an advantage'. Back in Waterford that evening I pulled out the atlas and found the group of islands, called the New Hebrides, which seemed to be roughly halfway between Fiji and Australia in the Coral Sea. The following day I put a phone call through to Elizabeth, rather fearing that the events of the last twenty-four hours would cause major disruption to her plans. During her first term at Dundee University she had found the course was orientated predominantly towards British maternal and child health and not terribly relevant to the problems in developing countries. Furthermore she had received letters from American friends whom she had made whilst working in Mwanza who had since returned to the United States of America. One in particular had taken up a post at his local university at Loma Linda in California, and offered Elizabeth a bursary to take a master's degree over there on a two-year course.

Without the benefit of a globe, and working solely from the flat page of an atlas, we assumed that the New Hebrides islands could not be very far from California, and so I went ahead and submitted an application for this post to London. We were later to realise that the Pacific Ocean occupies roughly a quarter of the globe's surface and so in fact there was a vast distance to travel between these two places. Within two weeks Elizabeth had returned to Waterford and I was summoned to London for an interview at the headquarters of the Overseas Development Ministry based in Eland House near Victoria Station. I was immediately put at my ease by the Senior Medical Adviser who himself had worked in Uganda for many years, and he explained the background to the post that was currently being advertised.

The New Hebrides comprises a group of some sixty islands stretched over 500 miles of the Pacific Ocean. Most of the islands are covered by areas of rainforest, and volcanic peaks rise steeply out of the ocean on most of the larger islands. The first settlers arrived in 1870 and in 1887 a Franco-British naval commission was appointed to ensure the maintenance of order and to protect people and their possessions. This was little more than a form of words at the time, but in 1906 a Franco-British condominium was formed with two Resident Commissioners, one British and the other French, with their official residencies on opposite sides of the newly-built part of the town of Port Vila. The police service, health service and education service were all duplicated, but now that the islands were approaching independence it had been deemed necessary to amalgamate these two colonial administrations.

All previous incumbents of the post of British government surgeon to the New Hebrides had been selected on the basis that they disliked the French, spoke no French, and were prepared to maintain the great 'divide'. Now the position had changed and the Overseas Development Ministry was anxious to identify a surgeon who spoke French and was prepared to work with the staff of the French Health Service there to amalgamate the resources into a unified health service for independence two years hence.

I pointed out to the interviewing panel that my last five years in Tanzania had been spent mainly in obstetrics and gynaecology and any general surgery had been restricted to the bowel and bladder. Nevertheless, I did hold the qualification of Fellow of the Royal College of Surgeons of Edinburgh. The interviewing panel had been informed that the French authorities had recently appointed a young surgeon fresh from his military service in Cambodia, with a wide background in trauma and thoracic surgery. With the planned integration of the health services our areas of experience would seem to complement each other well. I left the interview room and wandered round some of the London shops in search of suitable Christmas presents whilst the panel continued with the interviews. I returned to Eland House around four o'clock, as arranged, and there the Medical Adviser made me a formal offer of the position of government surgeon to the New Hebrides for a period of two years.

The run-up to Christmas that year in Waterford was concerned with packing up all our bits and pieces yet again. We arranged for heavy furniture items to be stored in England, along with the new Volvo estate car which we had purchased back in the summer. As we were now employees of Her Majesty's Foreign Service we had the luxury of professional packers to organise the dispatch of our chattels by air freight halfway round the world to the islands in the south-west Pacific. During the packing I came across two favourite rocking deckchairs that I had purchased from a carpenter in Masaka and noted that the canvas had rotted away and was in desperate need of renewal. I therefore made one last trip to the hardware store on The Quay.

'Do you have any deckchair canvas, please?'

'Are you not the man who came here in the August holidays wanting hot-water bottles?'

By now the whole store had stopped trading and was listening in to this conversation with great interest.

'Yes, indeed I am. But it was very cold in August even though it was the factory holidays.'

'And now with the winter gales blowing up the river you'll be wanting to sit out in deckchairs.'

I agreed. Any explanation would be hardly appropriate, especially as he was now halfway up the open staircase to the top floor where he kept his 'out-of-season' goods. He returned with two brightly coloured rolls of deckchair canvas, for which I thanked him. I took out my wallet but he declined any payment and wished me well.

'I've heard from the sisters up on the hill that you're leaving and wherever you're going and needing this sort of canvas then it would be a far more comfortable place than Waterford in the middle of winter. Goodbye now.'

# Chapter Nine

The fifth of January 1977 was a day that, as a family, we missed completely. It simply dropped right out of our calendar. There was a very long 4th January as we reported to Terminal Three at Heathrow at seven o'clock on a grey morning for our 9.30 Air New Zealand flight to Los Angeles and then on to Honolulu.

We arrived on the Hawaiian island well after dark, and so we missed seeing anything of the beaches, the volcanic peaks and the surf for which these islands are famous. We took off from Honolulu on the final leg of our long flight across the Pacific Ocean late on the evening of 4th January. Somewhere in the darkness we crossed the International Date Line and so we arrived at Nandi in Fiji in the mid-morning of 6th January.

Somebody in London had been thoughtful enough to book us into the airport hotel and so we were able to catch up on some sleep, enjoy some proper food and stretch our legs in the hotel gardens before getting a proper night's sleep. The following day we were booked onto the small jet service run by Air Pacific for the one-and-a-half-hour journey to Port Vila, the administrative centre of the New Hebrides islands.

The town was situated on the western shore of the island of

Efate, and as we approached from the south we could suddenly see the bright strip of golden sand that fringed the island and the dark green tropical rainforest that rose to cover the hills and occasional dramatic peaks. The beaches shelved into the almost turquoise shallow water that extended as far as the outer reef, beyond which the deep blue of the Pacific Ocean extended for miles.

We were met at the airport by the chief medical officer, a pleasant elderly Scot wearing a crisp white shirt, white knee-length shorts and long white socks. This form of dress, I was soon to learn, was favoured by most of the senior British expatriate staff. The French senior staff had a similar dress code in khaki, although the shorts were much shorter and the socks were often of ankle length. We were now in a colony with a Governor, referred to as the Resident Commissioner, who, on official occasions, wore his full white dress uniform topped by a white helmet with ostrich plumes. This presented a great contrast from the fiercely independent Tanzania that we had so recently left behind. Gone were the photographs of an African president in all public places and instead the Queen's picture appeared alongside that of the French president in every school, hospital and government office. The New Hebrideans, I was to learn later, assumed that this couple were married, as their photographs invariably appeared side by side in public. I was also to learn that New Hebrideans considered the one great advantage of being governed by two colonial powers was the inordinate number of public holidays during the year, with everything from the Queen's birthday to Bastille Day being marked by a day off work.

There are a dozen or so principal islands that form the New Hebrides, and at the time the population was 120,000 (roughly the size of the market town of Taunton). In addition to the two Resident Commissioners there were also two militia (police and security), two departments of education, two health services, and two administrations for the outlying islands. At least some progress had been made by the time we arrived with the judiciary. A French judge had been appointed who spoke good English, whilst the British judge was a Seychelloise, and he was also bilingual. Constitutionally, in the event of an irreconcilable problem arising that could not be solved by these two judges, the King of Spain was appointed as the arbiter.

French and English were the two official languages of the New Hebridean Condominium but the local people used Bislama, or Pidgin English, which was learnt by all the French expatriates as a foreign language. As a result they generally conversed better with the locals than did the British or Australian personnel working on the islands, who viewed the language as a corruption of English. The language evolved from the time that many New Hebrideans were taken to work on the sugar plantations in Queensland and the planters used a minimum of vocabulary and key phrases to communicate with their workers. Some French, some Spanish and some local words were also worked into this language. New encounters were incorporated into the language, often using small descriptive phrases rather than the internationally accepted noun. A brassiere was therefore referred to as a 'titi baskit', whilst an aeroplane was called a 'lorri go for uppa'. Rumour has it that when a piano first appeared on one of the islands it was called 'wun box imi gat black mo white teeth – time yu killim e sing sing'.

As a very civilised touch we were accommodated for the first two nights in one of the luxurious tourist beach hotels, as it was the weekend and we were certainly not expected to start work or move house until Monday. Sunday lunch at the hotel was a lavish buffet, and it was an opportunity to meet the French chief medical officer, who was there with his family. His wife, an elegant Tahitian lady, and their five daughters provided the cabaret with some very impressive Tahitian dancing, producing seemingly impossible hip rotations and flicks of the grass skirts. The music was provided by three young lads on guitars who we assumed to be part of the same family. Gordon, the chief medical officer, and his wife tut-tutted quietly throughout the performance as this was clearly not their perception of the role of a colonial chief medical officer and his family.

Just one week after our arrival Elizabeth left us, having booked herself to fly back across the Pacific to California to start her master's degree course at the start of the third week in January. She hoped to cover the first year's work within nine months, after which she would return for a short holiday on the islands. We had engaged the services of Violet, a young New Hebridean woman with her own two-year-old baby, who would clean, wash, iron and help out around the home.

Just after Elizabeth's departure we received a cyclone warning, as a large weather system was tracking its way across the Pacific from just south of Fiji and was expected to hit Efate Island at about eight o'clock in the evening. Our neighbours, the hospital superintendent and his wife, who both came from the central island of Ambrym (one of the three populated islands in the group with active volcanoes), had plenty of experience of these tropical storms. Frank explained to me that the local radio station, which normally closed down at nine o'clock each evening, would stay on air all night during a cyclone, transmitting details of the storm and giving its expected intensity and track. Both our houses were fairly recently built bungalows with huge picture-frame windows, which gave wonderful views over the hospital compound and down to the lagoon.

Sure enough the gale-force winds started to buffet the house in the late evening and the children and I opted for an early bed on the grounds that there might be disturbances during the night. I was woken at about two o'clock in the morning by some of the strongest winds I have ever experienced and I tuned in to the local radio station but I could find no reassuring voice, only static. Obviously this was a fierce storm to me but perhaps on the Pacific scale of cyclones it was possibly just a 'bad blow' and the radio staff had all gone off to bed. Within minutes the large windows on the south side of the house started to bend under the force of the wind and I hastily moved the furniture away from these windows fearing that the glass would shatter and driving rain would come pouring in. For the rest of the night the wind buffeted the whole structure of the bungalow which, thanks to its low profile, managed to withstand the forces of nature very well.

At first light the wind was still strong and horizontal rain was now the cause of the dominant noise as it pounded the windows. I put on a waterproof cape and virtually crawled to our next-door neighbour's house where Frank let me in and explained that the first severe gust of wind the previous night had blown down the radio transmitter and this was indeed a severe cyclone. He suggested that together we battle our way to the hospital to check the wards, casualty and general security. He warned me that the greatest danger was posed by sheets of corrugated iron that had been ripped off the roofs of local buildings and were now flying through the air at seventy miles an hour.

We reached the hospital and the nursing staff on duty reported that there was very little damage. In the planning phase, some five years earlier, the architect had been briefed to design a building capable of withstanding cyclones. As a result, the hospital units were all set into the hill which rose from the lagoon; all were single storey with low-pitched roofs and reinforced windows. The casualty sister, whose husband worked at the local radio station, informed us that we had been through what was locally termed a 'three black ball cyclone' which referred to a sign hoist on the main flagstaff in the port itself, as a tradition of the strength of the storm. Wind speeds of 120 miles an hour had been recorded during the night and she informed us that the eye of the storm would shortly be passing through the town and everything would then go calm for about an hour and a half. Coming from the Solomon Islands, she also had much experience of cyclones and expressed this stage in Pidgin English as 'wait fo backside lo storm cum tru'. Sure enough, the winds abated around ten o'clock that morning and it was possible to drive into town where everyone was scurrying around doing essential shopping, collecting mail, fresh bread and milk before rushing home again to wait for phase two. This started on cue at about noon, with the wind and rain returning with a vengeance. Then for the next eight hours the 'backside' of the storm blew through Efate, with strong winds this time on the northern side of the house.

The following day the cyclone had cleared right through the island and wandered off into the Pacific, leaving a trail of devastation in its wake. We drove out of town for a short way to look at the effects of the storm, and saw the coconut plantations that had been right in the eye of the storm. A swathe roughly 100 metres wide had been cut through the plantations, and the trees in this corridor had been completely uprooted and felled. Trees in the adjoining areas of the plantation were bent and twisted but probably still viable. One of the small local beaches had been denuded of all its sand where the wave and wind direction had obviously combined to lift all the fine sand, leaving a surface of bare rocks and mud.

I drove on to the French hospital to meet André, my counterpart, and see how they had survived the storm. Their hospital was also fairly new but had been erected on flexible foundations to cope with earthquakes and tremors. The New Hebrides islands are situated on a geological fault line, with two or three minor tremors each month affecting one or more of the islands. Fortunately, violent tremors are rare but two recorded events in 1927 and 1965 caused significant damage in Port Vila. The staff at the French hospital said that the storm had produced a feeling similar to being on a liner in a gale at sea, with the building swaying in different directions as the winds moved around, but they had also escaped any significant damage.

The children quickly settled into the British primary school which was situated just ten minutes' walk from the hospital compound on the edge of the cricket square. Violet arrived in good time each morning to walk the children to school, practising her English during the journey. The first few days at school were devoted to earthquake and cyclone drill which was held with all the intensity of the school fire drills in Waterford. If a sudden cyclone came through the islands then you went under your desk and lay there until the all clear sounded. If an earthquake was the signalled danger then you rushed outside to the centre of the cricket square and lay down. The British expatriate population were outnumbered by the Australians and New Zealanders, many of whom were representing commercial interests on the islands, as the British and French authorities had agreed a tax-free status for any company based on the islands and also for any shops trading in the port area.

After his second day at school Jonathan, then aged five, came home and I asked the usual parental question, 'How was school today?'

Without too much thought he replied 'Oh, all right thanks. What's a pommie bastard?'

He then fell to discussing how unfair it was that the boy in the desk next to him, who came from Fiji, was able to move each of his toes individually when he had kicked off his sandals. This meant that he could do the maths problems very quickly with the advantage of counting on both his fingers and his toes.

Claire was very anxious for a pet of some sort and we decided that a kitten would be a good first step in this direction. Violet informed us that the big supermarket in the town, which was owned by a Vietnamese family, had a family of cats in their store area to keep vermin under control and were often happy to give a kitten to a good home. As there was no school on Saturday mornings, Claire and I took advantage of the first opportunity to combine a shopping trip with the hopeful acquisition of a kitten. All the big retail businesses in Port Vila at that time were run by Asians. Many Chinese came in with British passports from Hong Kong, whilst a large Vietnamese community arrived after the French withdrawal from their country. I asked to speak to the manager of the supermarket to explain my request.

'You want cat?'

'Yes please, a small one if possible. A kitten.'

'Okay. Black cat okay?'

'Yes fine. Can we see it?'

We were taken into the storeroom, squeezing between the packing crates and boxes, until he pointed to a small old box with several furry bundles in its base. Claire chose a little black kitten, and the manager found a small container in which we could carry it home. For the next twenty-four hours this kitten displayed incredible agility, climbing up all the curtains, swinging on the pelmets and the light fixtures, and generally defying any notion of being domesticated. On the Sunday morning we returned to the supermarket and asked to speak to the Vietnamese manager again. He was moderately understanding about our problem.

'Ah! You want cat for house?'

'Yes, but we want the cat to be quiet and to get used to the house.'

'Ah. So cut whiskers and put butter on paws and cat will be very quiet.'

We followed these instructions and the transformation was remarkable. Pinkle Purr as she was called, curled up in Claire's lap and shunned the highlife and trapezes around the house completely.

One of my first expatriate patients during that early time at Port Vila was one of the senior veterinary officers, who was admitted to hospital with severe renal colic, which we discovered (following an X-ray) was being caused by a stone tracking down from his left kidney. After much spasm and sweating the stone was then noted to be lodged in the bladder, from where it refused to budge. His contract terms covered a medical evacuation by air to his home country of New Zealand, but fearing the discomfort of the journey and the upheaval to his family he asked if it were possible to remove it in Port Vila under a general anaesthetic. Using an endoscope passed into the bladder, I could find the calculus relatively quickly, and with a pair of long forceps I was able to crush the stone. The bits and pieces were then flushed out and the young vet was able to return home the following day.

A couple of days later I received a note through the door at home expressing his appreciation and indicating that his little bitch had just had a litter of puppies. As they were due to be weaned soon he wrote that if we would like to have the pick of the litter we would be most welcome. I collected the children from school the following afternoon and drove to the vet's house, where we were greeted by a cacophony of barking from the proud parents, who turned out to be two smooth-haired black and tan dachshunds. A basket of four puppies presented a most difficult problem for the children as each little pup seemed to have something special. At last a decision was made and the larger of the two female puppies was chosen, cuddled, and carried very carefully to the car.

Once home the discussion started on selecting a name; eventually a nostalgic choice was made and a Swahili name was bestowed on the unsuspecting puppy. 'Fupi' means short legs in Swahili, and this seemed to be approved by a majority decision. Yet another dachshund in the house, and this made the home feel very familiar.

With most aspects of everyday life throughout the islands divided into British and French sectors, it was hardly surprising to find that recreational activities were similarly split. The main administrative building of the British Residency looked out over the cricket square (but on the opposite side to the primary school) where Aussies, Kiwis and even the occasional Irishman joined the British putting bat to ball most weekends and late afternoons. The French boasted a grand sports arena with a track suitable for cycling and running, whilst their Residency was surrounded by a sandy area under the shade of mature palms where pétanque was played after working hours.

With so many beaches to choose from on the island of Efate, it was hardly surprising that some of these were also segregated in an unofficial way. The 'British beach' was a delightful stretch of sand just three miles from our hospital with a well-developed inner coral reef which allowed very safe swimming amongst beautiful coral pools. A beach hut was provided as a place in which to change, or even shelter in the event of a sudden tropical downpour, and whilst French families and New Hebrideans were not exactly excluded, none chose to use the facilities. The French would drive a few extra kilometres for more seclusion and a bit of natural sunbathing. Even among the French community there were some subdivisions, as evidenced by a roadside sign to the Breton beach. Once a year the Bretons organised a superb barbecue with live music and extended an open invitation to the Welsh, Irish, Cornish, and bagpipe-playing Scots for what was rated the best Celtic al-fresco occasion of the year.

We contented ourselves with the safety and conventional swimming attire of the British beach simply because of its proximity to our house and the safe bathing in the coral pools for the children. One Saturday afternoon on returning to my shorts and towel I found that my wrist watch had been stolen from the pocket of the shorts. None of the other families on the beach had seen anything suspicious, but realising that such an event in East Africa meant that one would never see the watch again, I contented myself with the knowledge that I was fully insured for such losses. Knowing that we were working in a duty-free port and that I would be able to replace the watch with a much more sophisticated model on my 'new for old' policy, the theft was not particularly upsetting.

The following day I confidently went into Fung Kwei, a large duty-free camera and watch store in the town, and chose a replacement watch. Looking at my insurance policy that evening I realised that the theft had to be reported to the local police station, so early the next day I went along to speak with the British station sergeant.

'Do not worry, Doctor, we will find your watch today,' he calmly informed me once I had given him all the details of the theft.

'But I have no idea who stole the watch, or even when it was taken exactly,' I replied.

'But you see, Doctor, there was another theft yesterday on that beach,' the sergeant continued, 'in fact the Resident Commissioner had his shorts stolen around lunchtime, and his false teeth were in the pocket. Now the Resident Commissioner has to address the National Assembly tomorrow, and he cannot speak without his teeth. So all police leave has been cancelled and, as we are speaking, a large police force is now conducting a house search of the villages in that area.'

Sure enough I received a message later that afternoon to confirm that my watch had been found and, more importantly, a pair of shorts with a set of dentures in the pocket had also been recovered. I scrapped the insurance claim and contented myself in the knowledge that at least I could take my old watch on future swimming expeditions.

The French held the monopoly on good horse riding on the island of Efate with their 'Club Hippique' set within a large coconut plantation on the eastern shore of the island. Having been introduced to horse riding during our short time in Waterford, the children were anxious to continue riding and André gave me information about the children's afternoons which the club organised. We made a booking for several sessions, which gave great pleasure and excitement to Claire and Jonathan, and the professional expertise and teaching of the riding school were obviously of a very high standard. Chatting about the riding club with colleagues in the hospital gave us an idea to form a group who would join together in a 'staff trek' one Saturday afternoon. The horses and the guide were duly booked, and as it turned out all the members of our group were male. We were introduced to the trek guide, who was a young instructor called Monique; she then in turn introduced us to our horses.

We set off from the club paddock and we were soon riding along a narrow track under the coconut palms, with high grasses on either side. Once we were well established on this track Monique, who was on the lead horse, took off her T-shirt and gave a whole new meaning to 'bareback riding'. Every so often she would half turn around to call out instructions or to check on progress, but our horses seemed so well schooled that they refused to even catch up with the lead horse let alone have a chance to get alongside. It certainly made for an interesting ride and Stuart, the hospital pharmacist, vowed that he had never tried so hard to spur a horse forward before, but all to no avail. After two hours of riding on picturesque but narrow pathways the club buildings came into view and Monique slipped her shirt back on just as the track opened up in order to allow the trek to ride into the home paddock two or three abreast – so to speak.

The New Hebrideans gave only limited allegiance to the colonial recreation pursuits. Most of the young men chose instead to indulge in football on every piece of spare ground and every level patch of sandy beach. The French-speaking teams generally had better kit and equipment than their English-speaking compatriots. The British Hospital team had only recently been formed and, watching from the touchline for their first game of the year, I noticed that most of our team only had one boot. It transpired that the football squad had played barefoot for many years but recent allocation of funds had allowed them to purchase just six pairs of boots. The goalkeeper had the luxury of a pair of boots, in order to improve his clearances, whilst the other team members had one boot each, which hopefully was not only the right size but also fitted the dominant foot. In spite of the rough coral surface of the roads most of the young New Hebrideans wandered around quite happily without shoes or sandals.

Violet, our home help, walked up from her village by the lagoon each morning barefoot and walked the children to school without the luxury of shoes. She wore the traditional 'Mother Hubbard' dress which so many of the women on all the islands of the New Hebrides wore. This garment had been introduced by the missionaries in the 1880s to cover up the nudity of the local girls and young women. This was the popular style among European women of that time with its puffed sleeves, high waist and full skirt, and the pattern of dress remained as a 'respectable outfit' for generations of New Hebridean women. The missionaries fared less well with the men, and although on the main island of Efate the men wore shorts and a shirt, on many of the outer islands the men still wore the traditional *nambas*. This was essentially a penis cover made out of woven banana fibre, rather like a rigid condom, and fixed in place with a wide waistband of banana fibre.

On many of these islands the women and young girls wore grass skirts made from plain dried and unstained strands of local grasses rather than the 'Mother Hubbard'. Occasionally these would be set alight as the very young wearer strayed near an open cooking fire, and horrendous burns were often inflicted. Some of the girls, usually of the French-speaking community, played cricket, a game which was strangely very popular with women in the neighbouring French colony of New Caledonia, where at that time it was the women's national sport. The actual bats were made with a long curved piece of wood and even in New Caledonia the 'Mother Hubbard' was the traditional costume in which to play cricket among the ladies' teams.

With the administration of these islands divided into four districts, it was suggested that I should visit at least one of these districts at an early stage in my tour of duty, in order to appreciate the facilities available at the small district hospitals. The District Medical Officer for the southern part of the New Hebrides was based on the island of Tanna, and he had been in post for nearly a year at that time. Richard was a medical graduate of Edinburgh University and had worked for a couple of years in Zambia before taking up this position on Tanna. His location was probably one of the most interesting in the group, as the island not only boasted an active volcano but also possessed some spectacular scenery and wonderful beaches.

Tanna was one of the first islands in the New Hebrides to be converted to Christianity by the Presbyterians, and during the Second World War the island was used extensively in the build-up for the battle of Guadacanal in the Solomon Islands in 1944. In the two years prior to this battle to dislodge the Japanese from their foothold in the Pacific, the American forces built a sizeable landing strip on the flat area in the centre of the island and identified several large bays with natural harbours for their supply ships to anchor close to shore. As a result of these troop movements many of the local people left the coastal villages and mission stations to return to their ancient villages in the hilly terrain of the interior of the island. Throughout 1943 and the early part of 1944 a large American airlift made a dramatic impact on the whole island. Huge transport aircraft flew in troops and supplies throughout the daylight hours and local cattle, hens and other livestock were purchased in the early days from the islanders. New buildings were erected and refrigerators, freezers, air conditioners and cookers all arrived on the island, powered by the military generators.

One of Richard's local medical assistants, who was nearing his retirement from government service, told me of his memories during those heady days in Tanna when the Americans were preparing for their assault on the occupied Solomon Islands. Up to that time he pointed out that the islanders' only contact with outsiders was restricted to doctors, nurses, teachers and missionaries. Now vast numbers of American soldiers were stationed on the island. The local Tanna people continued to harvest their taros or yams, which they then pulverised and mixed with coconut milk before wrapping the 'mash' in banana leaves and cooking it in an earth oven for several hours. This then formed the local staple of *lap-lap*. The finished article resembled thick mashed potato and meals were then served as a sandwich of meat or fish between the two pieces of *lap-lap*. With the arrival of the Americans, and their enforced purchase of all local livestock, fresh meat became very scarce and the Americans therefore provided tins of corned beef to the local communities, which were rapidly assimilated into the dietary pattern. This processed meat could be thickly sliced and placed between the layers of *lap-lap*.

William indicated that this all worked very well for a few months and the local Tannese were more than happy with the free provision of processed meat. The arrival of a new military medical officer on the base focussed attention on footwear and he felt that all the local people should wear shoes. William remembered the day that a large consignment of rubber flip-flops arrived, all dark pink in colour, and were distributed to the local people without any instructions. As a young teenager William vividly remembers the first evening that the rubber thongs were incorporated into the *lap-lap* and the old men, who always laid first claim to any new delicacy, chewed late into the night on these sandwiches made from rubber flip-flops before giving up and going up to search for some dried fish in the food store.

At the end of the war the island of Tanna suddenly became strangely quiet without all the American serviceman. It was then that a 'cargo cult' grew up in many areas of the island, which was known as the John Frumm Movement. One explanation of this name is that it was the name of an American quartermaster sergeant who was responsible for issuing supplies to the locals, often with only limited communication possible. The islanders had returned to their local native communities, and instead of the Presbyterian teaching they followed the Movement of John Frumm. They cherished the belief that further ships and aircraft would come to the islands bringing corned beef, cans of food, refrigerators, jeeps, Coca-Cola and all the other trappings of American society. Those villages believing in John Frumm marked their cult following with a large wooden red cross painted on a board in a prominent position in the village. Great efforts were made by local government officers to convince such villages to relinquish this belief, and some headway was starting to be made when a royal visit to the New Hebrides took place. It was decided that the Duke of Edinburgh would fly into Tanna for a short visit on his own, leaving the Queen in Efate for the day. Schoolchildren were all lined up in clean clothes, the local police were on parade in crisp uniforms and many flags were issued just before the gleaming royal plane flew in and landed with much ceremony. As the Duke departed a huge feast was laid on and food presents were distributed as a token of goodwill. After this visit a splinter John Frumm group became established honouring the Duke of Edinburgh, and his photo was displayed in all houses in these villages, which also continued to sport the large red wooden cross.

After a day spent in Richard's district hospital we set off early the next morning to climb the active volcano of Yasur at the eastern point of the island. We drove to the foothills and then climbed as far as was safe up the steep slides of pumice stone through which sulphurous fumes and smoke seeped out. Once the rumbling of the volcano became louder and pieces of red lava started spinning down the slope towards us, we decided that we had climbed far enough. To go any further without protective gear was not advisable so we turned and clambered down to the vehicle. We then found a local beach of black 'volcanic' sand and had a most welcome swim to get the dust and smell out of the system. I realised that my integration period in the New Hebrides was now over and that a spell of hard work beckoned.

## Chapter Ten

From my first few weeks in Port Vila I was aware of a strong following for herbal medicine. Whereas in East Africa the local medical practitioners indulged in a variety of witchcraft, hypnotism and suggestive 'voodoo' in combination with herbs, the local doctors of the islands seemed to content themselves by using the rich vegetation available in the bush and tropical rainforest for most of their remedies.

During the months of April and May several species of fish, including the popular and tasty parrott fish, were attracted to the inner reefs where the coral was in bloom. At such a time the Cigua toxin is produced by the bacteria inside the tiny reef organisms. As a result of this the toxin enters the food chain and certain species of fish can become poisonous for a short period. Eating such fish causes a feeling of faintness accompanied by vomiting and sweating, and this is followed by diarrhoea.

Parrott fish was plentiful and had a good flavour so it appeared regularly on the dinner tables in Port Vila and other towns. Many hostesses followed the local practice of feeding some of the fish intended for the evening meal to the house cat during the afternoon to monitor the effects. To the cat the poison was unpleasant and was usually vomited back promptly, so it seldom had severe or fatal effects. With the pressures of entertaining one hostess forgot all about the 'cat test' until the guests were arriving. She hastily removed the fish from the oven and fed a piece to the grateful cat just as the guests sat down to dinner. They were about to start the fish course when the cat appeared, arched its back, and threw up in front of the guests. The fish course was immediately removed from the dinner table.

Late one evening in that first April I was called to the maternity unit where a mother was having problems with a breech delivery, and having achieved a successful outcome I was passing by the casualty department when I saw an Australian couple on the trolleys there looking very ill. On questioning, the staff nurse revealed to me that they were both suffering from fish poisoning. They were very pale, sweating and occasionally vomiting, but also becoming increasingly more confused. The duty casualty officer had intravenous lines running and had given them atropine, which was the considered drug of choice. The staff nurse suggested that she might try a preparation of leaves from a plant that grows on the edge of the lagoon and I encouraged the casualty officer to at least give this treatment some consideration. The nurse scurried off with a torch to collect the all-important leaves and returned after about fifteen minutes. These were then crushed before being infused in boiling water, and the liquid was administered to the patients by mouth once it had cooled sufficiently.

Both patients then recovered well over the next ten minutes but were kept in hospital overnight as a precaution before being allowed home early the next day. I asked the staff nurse if there was a good local practitioner who lived in the area, and she indicated that the New Hebridean housing estate close to the hospital was where the best local 'doctor' lived and practised. She promised to arrange an introduction for me in the fullness of time.

The return to general surgery was not quite the shock to the system that I had anticipated. I had spent the previous six years in the speciality of obstetrics and gynaecology, with occasional surgery procedures involving the large bowel or bladder. I reasoned to myself that the Vila Base Hospital would be like Kitovu Hospital in Uganda but on a larger scale, and for 90% of the time this was true. The great problem concerned those patients who needed surgical intervention in an area where I was not experienced and, as a last resort, we did have an option of airlifting a patient for specialist surgery to our nearest centre of excellence in Brisbane, some 1,500 miles away. The cost of such a procedure was prohibitive and therefore we were encouraged to carry as much as possible at a local level.

In this respect I was indeed fortunate to have André, the French surgeon, as a colleague, and his support was invaluable. His training had been as an orthopaedic surgeon and this, coupled with experience in trauma whilst serving with the French forces in Cambodia, meant that he had a very wide surgical experience. Added to this was the fact that emergency admissions from the other islands tended to arrive only during the hours of daylight. This meant that life was much more structured, and contact with the French hospital on a daily basis allowed for an exchange of views on any emergency admissions. In Africa a party carrying a sick or injured relative would think nothing of driving or walking through the night to seek medical help and would often arrive at the hospital doorstep in the middle of the night. In the New Hebrides the transport of patients between islands took place using light aircraft (or small boats), and with no landing lights on the outer islands patients were evacuated to Port Vila only during the hours of daylight.

So it was that just four months into my tour of duty a little girl was flown in from the island of Malekula. The story was that whilst playing on the rocks at low tide she had slipped, fallen backwards and gashed the back of her head. She complained of a severe headache and was losing consciousness at times. An X-ray confirmed that she had suffered a depressed fracture of her skull, and I showed a picture of the piece of bone that was pressing on the brain to her parents and tried to explain the situation through an interpreter.

Each of the islands of the New Hebrides had a different language, and few of the local people outside the towns understood

Bislama. On the larger islands, where communities were isolated by mountain ranges or strong coastal features, several languages existed. Usually it was possible to find a nurse in the hospital who came from near the village and the island involved, and we were fortunate enough to obtain a translator for Rose's parents. As we talked I noticed that Rose had developed a strange palsy of her eye muscles, and each eye seemed to drift downwards and outwards. This indicated that the fine nerves supplying these muscles had become involved in the swelling and increased pressure around the fracture site.

André came over from the French hospital to examine her with me and then joined me in a surgical venture to open her skull and elevate the depressed fragment of bone that was causing the problem. A stable anaesthetic was essential as any sudden involuntary movement or cough could result in brain damage. I helped the medical assistant to put Rose to sleep with an intravenous injection of a short-acting barbiturate and then administered a muscle-relaxing injection to paralyse the little girl. It was then possible to put a tube into her trachea, after which the medical assistant was able to give the anaesthetic gases through this main airway to maintain a good stable anaesthetic. André and I then lifted a flap of scalp and bored two holes using a trephine on either side of the fracture site. Then, using a hand-held saw (resembling the blade of a fretsaw) inserted through one of the trephine holes, a square window was cut in the skull bone, so allowing us to raise the depressed fragment of bone with only minimal damage to the brain tissue underneath. A small stainless steel 'skull cap' was then fitted into place to cover the defect and the flap of scalp sewed back. Little Rose had a stormy few days after surgery, during which time we had to keep her well sedated, but at the end of the first week she was sitting up and talking with her parents. A further ten days saw her moving around the ward with confidence, and even her eyes had now started to return to normal. She then left the hospital with a happy smile on her face to return to her home island of Malekula.

Fractured skulls were relatively common on the islands of the New Hebrides, but fortunately most of the work went either to the vets or to the abattoir. Before the proliferation of offshore companies and tourism had attracted such interest from Australia and New Zealand, the economy of these islands was dependent on coconut plantations. These were established in the early 1900s using many of the flat coastal planes on the islands.

When the average coconut (as seen on the supermarket shelf) is enclosed in a large case of fibre and then bound by a thin woody coat, the weight of the nut comes to about seven or eight kilos. If this then drops from a height of twenty metres, the damage to any skull in the way will be both dramatic and severe. Coconut matting was traditionally made from the fibres around the actual nut, and at the same time copra, which is the sun-dried flesh of the coconut, was turned into livestock feed. After the Second World War the development of artificial fibres hit the market for coconut matting, and there was a similar slump in copra products as livestock feeds were developed from plant oils grown in Europe. However, it was found that the good soil base under the palms allowed certain grasses to grow well enough to sustain cattle. Thus a scheme was initiated in the late 1950s to cope with the many French colonials who had to leave Algeria. These businessmen and their families were sent instead to the Pacific islands, often with the inducement of generous aid and grants from metropolitan France. A ranching programme was set up underneath the coconut palm plantations, and so it was the cattle that suffered most from falling coconuts. Fortunately we received no human casualties whilst I was working at Port Vila, but I did have a chance to look at an X-ray taken two years previously where the poor victim's head resembled a hard-boiled egg that had been hit hard with a teaspoon.

The majority of our skull trauma was a result of fighting, usually triggered by the excessive consumption of cheap imported wine. The islanders had no tradition of making their own alcoholic beverages in the way that the Tanzanian people brewed *pombe*, which was a local beer made from bananas. In Uganda the local people consumed *waragi*, which was made from fermented sugar cane and passed through dangerous little stills in the villages to produce a vicious alcoholic spirit. Many of the New Hebridean islands produced either cava or a local variation of this brew. It was on the island of Tanna where we saw this being produced, and the starting ingredient is the root of a plant belonging to the pepper family. It was the duty of the young boys of the village to chew this root for considerable periods of time before spitting into a large container. This container was left to ferment for just one day, and in the heat and humidity fermentation took place rapidly. The effects of cava consumption, which produced many hallucinogenic problems combined with a strange detachment of the mind from the body, was down to the drug in the root, whilst the alcoholic content was probably fairly small. Certainly after three mugs of cava drunk at sunset most of the men eventually went into a deep sleep in the hut where the substance had been consumed. Cheap imported wines presented a much greater problem in the townships, often resulting in fisticuffs at the end of the evening.

Every so often the dental surgeon attached to the British hospital in Vila, who was a burly Fijian called George and whose frame would have graced the second row of any forward pack in New Zealand rugby circles, would go off on a real bender. Fortunately George was relatively law-abiding, even with a large load of alcohol on board, but it did mean that for the following twenty-four hours I would have to be responsible for any dental emergencies. As a rule, the great majority of these patients could wait, with the help of antibiotics and painkillers, until the expert's sobriety returned. A fractured jaw was a different matter altogether as this needed immediate attention. The inevitable happened at around eleven o'clock one evening when I received a call to go to casualty, as there was a patient with a fractured jaw.

The staff nurse on duty was apologetic but at the same time quite agitated as she pointed to the patient and said:

'*Imi Killim man blong Santo an imi gon lo Frennish Ospital.*'

Thinking that I not only had a fractured jaw to treat but a murderer as well, I started to share her agitation and questioned her further. It transpired that the word *killim* in Bislama means to hit with force and if that force renders the object of the aggression dead then the expression used is *killim finis*. I suggested that we called in the theatre staff and prepared this patient for surgery. The upper part of his jaw had escaped damage but the lower jaw, or mandible, had a clean break and the only way of immobilising and supporting this fracture was to wire the upper and lower jaw together.

Working in the mouth meant that the anaesthetic tube had to be passed up one nostril and down the back of the throat before entering the trachea or windpipe. Whilst theatre was being opened I took advantage of half an hour with a textbook on operative surgery just to revise the various stages in the operation, knowing that André was busy at the French hospital with my patient's assailant. Stainless-steel wire was looped around every tooth on the upper and lower jaw and twisted firmly, and then finally the fixing wires were inserted between the corresponding teeth on the upper and lower jaws, thus locking the bones in position, hopefully for a period of at least six weeks. Fortunately my patient had lost a tooth in an earlier fight and so he was able to insert a large straw through which to take sustenance during the post-operative period.

The following Saturday we returned from a lazy afternoon at the beach with slightly shrivelled skin from spending so long snorkelling in the pools, taking in the brilliant colours of all the fish and coral. A message awaited me, asking me to go over to casualty as there was a patient there with a severe fracture to his thumb. The children were happy enough to read after the long day of swimming, and I went over to the hospital and found that the patient, a sixty-five-year-old Englishman, had been given some sedation for the pain in his thumb, which was indeed fractured just close to the wrist. I explained to him that the only reliable method of stabilising the break was to insert a stainless steel wire into the bone, leaving the end protruding through the skin. After the usual Plaster of Paris application for a few weeks, this wire could then be removed without another anaesthetic once X-rays had confirmed good bone union. Peter agreed to this and we arranged to take him to the operating theatre that evening to fix the problem.

His wife, who spoke with a broad Yorkshire accent, unlike her husband's rather precious style of English, was a bit concerned. They ran a big pig farm on a plateau in the hills above Efate and she would need to organise some help during the coming weeks when her husband's right hand would be out of action. She left her husband in our care and went off before dark to arrange for men to come in the following day. She returned on the Sunday to collect her husband and invited us as a family to come and see their farm the following weekend. It turned out to be a large and well-run enterprise in which they were both very actively involved.

Peter explained that five years previously he had suffered a severe stroke whilst living in Barnsley and working as Managing Director of a local company. He had lost the use of his right side and was unable to speak. After weeks of intensive physiotherapy he managed to get himself walking again and regained the use of his right hand but his speech was still very poor. He retired from the company and took all his savings out to the New Hebrides to buy this plot of land and establish a pig farm. They brought out with them books on pigs and relied on the knowledge and affinity of the local people with these animals to overcome their areas of ignorance in this venture. Working on the farm every day strengthened his right side and each evening he sat down to listen to one of the many records of John Gielgud reading Shakespeare that he had brought out with him, at the suggestion of his speech therapist. After he had played a part of the record he then tried to imitate what he had just heard. Two years of listening to and then copying the maestro resulted in a speech that was almost perfect, but he sounded just like John Gielgud with his pronunciation and phraseology. His wife told me that when they had gone home on leave to see their family in Yorkshire one year previously, all the relatives had just burst out laughing whenever they heard Peter speak. Happily his thumb healed well and once he was out of plaster, with the wire removed, he was able to return to his beloved pigs after an enforced absence of six weeks.

The following month, again as a result of a drunken fight, a patient was brought into the hospital but was pronounced dead on arrival. The Superintendent of Police paid a visit to the hospital the next day and requested me to carry out a post-mortem examination. I scurried around to see if any of the other four doctors in the hospital that day had any experience of conducting such an examination, but I was informed that, as the British surgeon, it was part of my duty. I was then ushered through to the small mortuary attached to the hospital, and there the tools of the trade were all laid out by the mortuary porter. Fortunately he had seen these examinations carried out over the last ten years and was able to put the right instrument into my hand at each stage of the procedure. With the history of a fight in an otherwise seemingly fit middle-aged man, we proceeded straight to the skull and, using a stainless steel saw, I was able to lift off the vault of the skull. A large fracture of the base of the skull immediately became apparent, and the brain damage around this was obvious. A cursory examination of the chest cavity confirmed that the heart and lungs were normal, and the abdominal examination also showed no damage to the organs there.

I was requested to present my evidence at the inquest three days later and was impressed by the courteous and co-operative manner in which both the French and the British judges handled the situation. Each seemed to have a good working knowledge of the other's language. The court interpreter allowed the New Hebrideans to present their evidence in Bislama, and this evidence was then relayed in French or English to the judges. My post-mortem findings were given to the court and the accused was subsequently found guilty of murder and sentenced to fifteen years in custody.

One hesitates to use the word 'prison'. Even the term 'open prison' would have been a bit of an overstatement for the jail on Efate. A rough fence marked the boundary of the prison farms and buildings, and a driveway of white painted stones led to the guardhouse. Visiting prisoners was on an 'ad hoc' basis, usually through a gap in the fence during a lull in farm work. Children waved to the prisoners on their way to school and relatives often passed snacks through the fence during meal breaks. When I questioned the Superintendent of Police about the laxity of security he assured me:

'Everyone knows what they have done and that they are being punished. If they did walk through the fence then where would they go? You see, this is a small island and everybody knows what is going on.'

Certainly during my time on Efate there were no breakouts, and in fact one prisoner requested an additional three months on his sentence as he wished to harvest the yams that he had planted on the prison farm in order to take them home.

My experience and background in gynaecology brought referrals and recommendations from André at the French hospital, and I quickly discovered that my enhanced O Level French did not extend to gynaecological terms. I now took to consulting with a dictionary under my desk so that I could follow the expressions used by many of the French women to describe the misery of the menstrual cycle. My French was further compromised by the attendance, in one clinic, of the wife of the English judge, who was a French-speaking Seychelloise.

She calmly asked me in English: 'Could you please give me something so that my husband does not have to wear socks in bed at night?'

Now at that particular time of the year the nights were so hot and humid that even a sheet felt like a blanket, so I surmised that anyone who had to wear socks in bed must have severe circulatory problems. I suggested to her that she should persuade her husband to come and see me, but she insisted that this was a matter for the wife. At long last I realised that the term 'socks in bed' was French Seychelloise slang for what we call a French letter and what the French refer to as a *caput anglais*. With the religious affiliation of the French hospital towards the Roman Catholic Church, many of the French wives came to the British hospital for oral contraception to be prescribed.

At that time many of the Australian and New Zealand staff on the islands spoke very little French, and the importance of being understood in this language was dramatically emphasised when our first elective medical student arrived from Melbourne University Medical School. Max had been a bit strapped for cash and so found the cheapest flight to the New Hebrides was via the neighbouring French island of New Caledonia. The terms of his cheap ticket indicated that he had to spend the Saturday night in the capital (Noumea) and he was delighted to find accommodation at a fairly cheap hotel. On his second day with us he was assisting me in an operating list and recounting how the language problem had really caused him no concern whilst he was in Noumea. He discovered that he only had to use the word 'oui' and was able to obtain all the food, drink and services he needed. Halfway through the operating list a message came to the theatre door that a member of the immigration staff from the airport wished to speak to Max about a young New Caledonian woman who had just arrived at the New Hebrides airport claiming to be the fiancée of our Australian medical student. After this Max hastily left the 'oui' out of his conversation again when sharing pleasures with young French-speaking ladies of the Pacific islands.

My French hit the buffers on one occasion during a dinner party at André's house towards the end of the school year, when traditionally the French wives and young children travelled to a small island just off the coast of New Caledonia. Here they spent four to six weeks relaxing at a beach club which organised special activities for various age groups of children. Priding myself that I knew the name of this location I confidently wished them a happy holiday on the Iles des Pines. The unfortunate point of this remark was that my pronunciation of the last word conveyed the sense of penises rather than pine trees and I left the dinner party to the sound of uncontrollable French mirth. André patted me on the back as I left and said that in his opinion my name for the island was probably more descriptive than the original, knowing the attitude of the young men who worked in the holiday camp through those months.

Just as I was about to head off into the housing estate next door to the British base hospital in search of the local practitioner who practised there, fate played a strange trick and I was informed that the 'local doctor' had been admitted to our hospital as an emergency. It turned out that he had been admitted under the care of the physician with severe jaundice, and subsequent tests confirmed that this jaundice was being caused by a gallstone which had impacted in his common bile duct, and therefore he was probably going to need surgery. I went to see him on the medical ward and found a man of about fifty-five who was completely bald and had a passable knowledge of English, as well as obviously being fluent in Bislama. I showed him the X-ray of his gall bladder and pointed out the numerous small gallstones and also drew his attention to the large gallstone which had blocked off the duct carrying the bile from the gall bladder and liver down into the intestine. I explained to him the need for surgery to remove his gallbladder and also to remove the stone that was causing the obstruction and the jaundice. He agreed to surgery and was then transferred over to the surgical ward, following which the operation was carried out the next day.

During his convalescence he joined me on daily ward rounds and took great delight in explaining how he treated the various fractures, abscesses and swellings that we saw. Indeed, it was obvious that many of the patients on the ward at that time had also consulted him on many occasions in the past, and they found that a joint ward round was a very interesting and amusing experience. Being a skilled bone setter, he was intrigued by the X-rays of fractures, and particularly those taken after reduction of the fracture. The majority of patients seeking his help with broken bones were given some local medicine to make them feel drowsy before he then set about reducing the fracture. Once he had re-established the bones in an acceptable position then he made his own splints out of carved strips of wood bound together with banana fibre. His results generally were very good as few of his patients needed to come to the hospital for further intervention.

I suggested to him that he might like to send his patients to the hospital for an X-ray after he had reset the fractures, and those that were acceptable would be returned to his care. Patients with non-aligned fractures or those people unfortunate enough to have a bone broken in several pieces would obviously be treated by the hospital, often with operative surgery using screws and metal plates. After his discharge from hospital he returned to his medical practice, and the arrangement for the X-ray facility continued to work well, to the advantage of both parties.

Shortly after this episode, one of the hospital staff sustained a horrendous compound fracture of his lower leg whilst playing football in a match for the hospital team against one of the French sides on a grass playing field adjoining one of the cattle-ranching projects. Daniel was one of our more dependable male nurses and came from the island of Tanna. He was brought into casualty with the bone ends sticking out through the skin and was in a great deal of pain. We took him to the operating theatre where, under a general anaesthetic, we scrubbed the bone ends clean of grass and dirt and then reduced the fracture before applying a thick back slab of plaster of Paris. This was standard practice for any compound fracture (one where the bone ends had broken the skin and so come into contact with the outside). This management allowed the natural swelling around the fracture site to settle down, in addition to facilitating inspection of the wound on a daily basis.

Towards the end of the first week the skin of the wound had started to heal well and the surrounding muscle was looking healthy, but there was a sinister swelling just above the wound. André came over from the French hospital to have a look at this with me and then had a look at the X-ray which had been taken that morning. This confirmed our worst fears, showing the presence of small gas bubbles in the muscles around the fracture site. It was obvious that Daniel had developed gas gangrene in his leg. André organised a special serum to be flown in from New Caledonia and we increased the dose of antibiotics, but the gas level palpably rose higher the next day. It was now possible to actually feel the gas in the tissues and in the calf muscles above the site of the compound fracture. André was insistent that the only way we could save this young nurse's life was to carry out an amputation at mid-thigh level, well above the level of the gas gangrene.

The agent responsible for this infection is one of the clostridium group of organisms which lie as spores in the soil for many years before entering a wound and then bursting into life to produce gas and high levels of toxin. I had only ever read of cases of gas gangrene in connection with the trench warfare of the First World War. André had treated patients with this complication during his military service in Cambodia and knew the importance of early radical surgery. Daniel was already showing signs of the toxic effect of these rapidly developing organisms, but was lucid enough to understand the sort of operation that was necessary and reluctantly agreed to its going ahead.

I always found amputations disturbing during my training in the operating theatre, but with the legs of diabetic patients or those with severe circulatory problems, where the toes or part of the foot becomes black with dry gangrene, then the sacrifice of the limb seems reasonable. Apart from the fracture and the large skin wound Daniel's leg looked normal enough from the outside, and this operation was very definitely the low point of my tour of duty in New Hebrides.

Daniel made a very good recovery from surgery and his stump healed well. We had a VSO radiographer working with us from Worthing in Sussex, and he had friends in Brisbane attached to the teaching hospital there. Alan was kind enough to contact them and give them all the details concerning Daniel's accident, the complications and the amputation. The hospital staff in Brisbane were incredibly generous and through local fundraising, combined with a donation from a Queensland charity, they organised Daniel's flight to Brisbane and his fitting with a colour co-ordinated leg in their artificial limb unit. He then spent six weeks in the physiotherapy unit at Brisbane learning how to walk again and was dispatched home with his artificial limb, along with a spare one in case of problems.

Tuberculosis is a disease which can affect almost any organ of the body, and during my time in East Africa I had encountered a number of cases of tuberculosis affecting the abdominal cavity, as well as the uterus and ovaries. It was never in my list of problem diseases in the New Hebrides, as these islands were sparsely populated and the standard of nutrition was good, with very little in the way of domestic overcrowding. It came as a complete surprise, therefore, towards the end of my first year in Port Vila when Don, the Australian consultant physician, asked me to assess a young patient on his ward. This thirty-year-old expectant mother from the island of Pentecost had been coughing up blood, and on chest X-ray she had tuberculous cavities at the apex of each lung. One of these cavities was bleeding and the amount was so copious that she had already received two blood transfusions. Clearly the tuberculous process had eroded a large blood vessel in one of these cavities, and it was important to determine from which lung the bleeding was coming. Under a light anaesthetic I passed a bronchoscope (which in those days was a rigid brass instrument) down her main airway to the point where the trachea divides, and sure enough the blood was gushing up on the left side, with no sign of any problem from her right lung.

André agreed to come round for the operation to remove the upper lobe of this young woman's left lung, and two days later we organised a thoracotomy (opening the chest through the bed of the fourth rib) in order to expose the diseased part of her lung. The whole operation took most of a morning to complete but the patient came through it well, with the help of seven units of blood donated by the local prisoners. Unfortunately, the young mother went into premature labour three days after the operation and the baby was too premature to survive. The patient herself made good progress and was discharged from hospital two weeks after the operation to return to her home island and to take appropriate antibiotics for the following two years.

The *entente cordiale* was not all one-way traffic, and on several occasions I went over to the French hospital to assist André with radical pelvic surgery for cancer of the cervix and also large bowel surgery. We were now working towards integrating the staff of all departments so that within a year or so we would have an single unified medical service. The British-trained nurses from our hospital went over to work on the wards of the French hospital and a list of drug names was prepared with the appropriate translations alongside. The only administrative problem arose when the British-trained nurses started to do the temperature round for the day and tried to get the patients to open their mouths to receive the thermometer. The patients themselves knew very well where the thermometer had been placed the day before by the French-speaking nurses checking their temperature, and kept their mouths tightly shut.

The islands of the New Hebrides offer the most wonderful sandy beaches, fringed with coconut palms, and lush tropical vegetation. The islanders living in the towns were totally at ease in the company of other races, whether Vietnamese, European or Australian, and this was a marked contrast to East Africa. Here the colonial history, both British and German, preceded by slavery at the hands of the Arabs, had caused a strong reserve and barrier to persist right through to the present day. Many of the young VSO workers or Peace Corps volunteers felt that they had 'crossed the divide' by having a local girlfriend. However, at the end of their assignment they returned to their home countries to further their careers and then their girlfriends were never really accepted back into the local group of young people.

By contrast, the hospital staff in the New Hebrides enjoyed beach picnics and barbecues as a group, and an afternoon on the seashore would often finish with a highly competitive game of volleyball in the early evening. It was within this social context of beach picnics that I was able to learn most from the nurses about island customs and beliefs.

Sand drawing was a technique practised by all children from an early age. In the damp sand of the ebbing tide intricate patterns were drawn with the index finger. The whole art form was committed to memory so that you could reproduce your own design faithfully and accurately each time it was drawn, without the index finger leaving the sand until the drawing was complete. The importance of this custom centred around the moment of your death when the soul leaves the body and makes for the seashore en route to the destination of one of the small uninhabited offshore islands where the souls of the departed assemble. To stop the evil one from following your soul across the water the sand drawing would be produced and the evil one would then have to copy this drawing exactly in the sand before following your soul. Thus, a complex pattern would produce a long enough delay for the soul to make its escape while the evil one struggled to reproduce an unfamiliar and intricate sand drawing.

Shark clapping was also widely practised on the beaches throughout the islands and the nurses took great delight in demonstrating this to the children during beach picnics. Traditionally it fell to the young teenage girls to ensure that the popular swimming beaches were kept safe for the small children and the boys. Using both hands, slightly cupped, to clap into the crest of the waves a hollow ringing sound was obtained. Whether it was actually this noise or the giggling and chatting of teenage girls which accompanied the practice that caused any sharks to keep their distance is a matter of debate. But despite the miles of coastline around these islands and the number of natural breaks in the outer reefs, the frequency of shark attacks reported each year seldom exceeded three or four.

It was during one of these beach picnics that two nurses from Pentecost Island encouraged me to plan to go to their home island to see the famous land jump, which was scheduled to take place in four weeks' time. They even offered to help me with the organisation of transport if I was able to get a small party together from among the hospital staff. They would plan the trip from Port Vila to the actual village where the jump was taking place and then back again on the same day. A few selected villages in the interior of the island take it in turns to stage these jumps each year. Whilst essentially the whole event is an initiation ceremony into manhood for those actually jumping, the origins of the tradition lie in a story concerning a young woman who was being forced into an arranged marriage. Running away from her intended and his friends, she came to the top of a vertical cliff. Carefully measuring the length of a strong local liana (vine) hanging from one of the trees, she tied one end to her ankle and the other to the stump of a tree. As her pursuers approached she threw herself off the cliff with a dramatic dive that took her to freedom and her own true love. These land jumps can only be staged during the two months of the year when the vines are old enough to be strong yet still young enough to be elastic. The villagers construct a high scaffold tower from wooden poles on the side of a steep hill to give a drop of some thirty to forty meters. Each participant is responsible for selecting and cutting his own lianas, and when his turn comes he dives head first from the top of the constructed platform to finish in the arms of his admirers and family at the foot of the hill. Prince Philip was privileged to witness one such jump during the royal visit to the islands, and following this the craze of bungee jumping seemed to become part of European and Antipodean culture.

Back at the hospital we organised a small group of redoubtable explorers who were prepared to set off from Vila Hospital well before dawn on the day of the jump. We boarded an Islander aircraft as the sun came up over the horizon, and landed on the island of Pentecost about an hour later. We had booked a local boatman for the journey from the landing strip to the bay nearest to the host village, which involved two hours' travel in what proved to be a choppy sea.

Our local guide met us off the boat and then led us through the dense tropical rainforest for about two hours until we reached the village with its scaffold tower, where the land jumping was already in progress. During our trek through the forest the humidity was so high and the canopy so dense that we lost all sense of direction and even the weather pattern was blotted out. Now, as we stood in the clearing, we could see and feel that it was raining and the ground underfoot was muddy and soft. Even so, the skill and courage of the young men jumping was beyond question. We could only spend just over an hour at the village before leaving with our guide to trek back through the tropical rainforest to our boat and then on to the flight back to Port Vila.

On most of the islands of the New Hebrides group personal wealth is assessed by the number of pigs that a man possesses. These are not the average domestic pig kept in a little pen close to the homestead but tusk-bearing creatures that roam freely throughout the garden area around the house. They are fed and generally fattened up for special occasions, but on reaching adulthood many bear quite sizeable tusks.

The senior New Hebridean doctor at the Vila base hospital had qualified at the South Pacific Medical School in Fiji soon after the end of the Second World War and was now nearing his retirement in the British Colonial Service. Marko had been awarded the MBE the year before I arrived, and I learnt a very great deal from him on local disease patterns and the attitudes towards Western medicine amongst the local population.

Marko's granddaughter was due to be married in a ceremony lasting several days, and as a family we were invited to the actual wedding ceremony in the church and the wedding feast afterwards. The week before the wedding Marko took me to his garden where he had special yams under cultivation for the feast, and I was surprised to find that their long tap roots go down for almost a metre and a half in the dry, hard-packed soil. Harvesting was thus a delicate and time-consuming business to extract these yams in their entire length and unbroken. Marko had to provide the pigs that would feed the guests at the wedding ceremony, but he had dispensed with the custom that demands the bridegroom actually kills the pig himself with a well-aimed blow to the centre of the animal's skull using a large wooden club. As a result the twisted ivory tusks from the recently dispatched boar that would traditionally have been worn in the lapels were replaced by a single white carnation buttonhole.

The pigs were cooked whole in a traditional earth oven. A huge pit is cut out, a good fire is lit at the bottom of the hole and large stones are then placed on the embers. The entire pig, wrapped in banana leaves, is lowered onto the stones. More stones are then used to cover the pig and the earth is replaced. Cooking time is about six hours, and during this interval the yams are grated and mixed with coconut milk to form the traditional *lap-lap*. This is then wrapped in banana leaves and cooked in similar earth ovens.

The church service, with tremendous community singing, took place at eleven o'clock in the morning and the wedding feast started at about one o'clock.

We were the first to leave at seven o'clock in the evening as dusk fell but we were aware that the singing and dancing would continue well into the following morning. At least we were privileged to drink French wine with the meal rather than cava out of gourds, so my mind remained clear. This was just as well, for at one stage I sat next to an elderly friend of Marko's who had worked for many years on the island of Malekula. Having talked about wedding feasts on his island he then went into the subject of funeral feasts, which were even more elaborate and lasted even longer. Cannibalism was still being practised in the days when he was working, but out of respect for the deceased rather than revenge on one's enemy. He recalled that in many parts of that island bits of the fingers of the deceased were added to the ceremonial stew so that members of the family could be assured of having taken a bit of their recently deceased relative into posterity. In the remote hill villages of Malekula, he explained, some tribes would wrap the body of the deceased in banana fibre ready for burial and then suspend it over the cooking area of the kitchen to 'lie in state', with the juices dripping down into the food.

There seemed little evidence that cannibalism had ever been practised on more than just a ritualistic basis in the New Hebrides. This was confirmed when we had a visit from Dr Gajdusek on his way back from Papua New Guinea to his base in California. This well-recognised research neurologist had been visiting the Fore people in the highlands of New Guinea, a tribe noted for practising cannibalism right up to the 1960s. The disease of *kuru* (which translates as 'shivering' in the Fore language) emerged about a hundred years ago and reached epidemic proportions in this small community in the 1950s. This was the first recorded incidence of Creutzfeldt-Jakob disease in humans, and Dr Gajdusek and others had spent a considerable time researching this condition and then publishing papers on its aetiology. As a result of feeding cattle with products containing animal protein (almost certainly brain and nervous tissue included) we now have the successor to *kuru* in the form of variant Creutzfeldt-Jakob disease (CJD).

The old Flanders and Swan song (*Eating people is bad*) has proved to be sadly prophetic.

# Chapter Eleven

My two-year contract in the New Hebrides still had some six months to run and as the '*entente cordiale*' with the French medical services was working so well the amalgamation of the two organisations seemed assured within a few months. I was therefore starting to cast around for ideas for future employment. Elizabeth was due to complete her master's degree a few months ahead of schedule, and during the one holiday when she had returned to Efate we took the opportunity visit New Zealand. John and Anna, our friends from Mwadui, had moved from Tanzania to work in Nelson on the South Island, and they extended a warm invitation to 'come and visit'. We enjoyed the experience of New Zealand, combined with some skiing, but were not sufficiently attracted to make it a working prospect, even though John and Anna and their family had obviously settled in very well.

Right out of the blue a telex came through to the Resident Commissioner's office asking me to fly out to London the following week for an important meeting. As so often with the civil service, all the details had been communicated to the chief medical officer before I was given any inkling of the reasons behind the request. I made an appointment to see Gordon in his office.

'I am sorry to appear curious, but perhaps you can inform me of the purpose of flying to London next week at such short notice.'

A rather curt response was my reward.

'It is all very inconvenient for the health service here and you are under no compulsion to go on this trip. It would seem that the medical adviser wants you back at headquarters for two days of meetings and then to join a party going out to Tanzania on a fact-finding tour.'

'That sounds like quite a time away from the islands,' I replied.

'Quite so, very inconvenient,' was the gruff reply.

'Is this just an evaluation study or is there the likelihood of a job in Tanzania in the near future?'

'I really could not express any opinion on that!' came the response.

This was Gordon's last tour before retirement and he really wanted two things: as little to do with the French and as few 'ripples in the pool' as possible. My temporary absence would threaten him on both fronts. I asked him to telex Murray that I would be in London, as requested, and asked him to authorise the residency office to book me a return air ticket.

I mentioned the trip to Frank, the medical superintendent, and received a much more enthusiastic response.

'I am sure that André will come over and operate on any emergency patients whilst you are away.' He then thought for a moment and added, 'As we are neighbours, would Claire like to come and stay with us whilst you are away? She can always go back to your house for books and homework – Anna would love to have her to stay, and she is so good with our girls.'

I thanked Frank for his understanding and generous offer, and as word of my trip went around the hospital the theatre sister offered to have the boys to stay with them as her son was in Jonathan's class at school.

The medical adviser in London was now able to communicate with me directly and a telex arrived giving me more details of the trip and the suggested project. It seemed that a large government aid project to Tanzania was in the pipeline and the Tanzanian Minister of Health had asked for me by name to head the programme.

Gossip is usually rife in any expatriate community but none more so that on a small island, and that evening the wife of the Deputy Resident Commissioner, whom I had met on no more that one or two occasions, called round to the house.

'I heard that you are leaving for London in a few days and then going out to Dar es Salaam on a feasibility study, so I wonder whether you would be kind enough to take this parcel out to my parents who live in Dar?'

'Well, yes. Certainly.'

'I will write to my father and he will call around late next week to the High Commission there and collect it from the mail office.'

Somehow I could not refuse. Communication with family in England was difficult enough from these isolated Pacific islands, but for this lady's family in Tanzania the problems must be even greater.

The first leg of my journey was across the Coral Sea to Brisbane, and as we entered Australian air space the cabin staff walked the length of the aircraft with two aerosol sprays on full blast, causing all the passengers to cough violently. All this, they assured us, was to protect Australia from foreign insects. They then handed out immigration cards and customs forms. A sense of self-protection came over me as I read through the list of prohibited imports and I decided to inspect the contents of the lady's parcel. As I feared it contained a mass of jars, preserves, tinned foods and sundry dried delicacies, the majority of which were featured on the customs sheet. I decided to make a clean breast of the problem and perhaps try to obtain substitutes at a good Asian food market in London.

We disembarked into the bright sunshine of a Brisbane morning and I breezed into the customs hall and went to the section for transit passengers. A stocky little Australian customs officer in white shorts and long white socks stood behind the table and I placed my hand luggage in front of him.

'Good morning,' I said. 'I have to tell you that I seem to have nearly everything on your list of prohibited items with the exception of the last paragraph that says "Hair, Semen and Feathers", and I have even got two of those.'

The customs officer looked at me and mouthed 'Stupid Pommie git' before scrawling a chalk mark on my baggage and waving me through for the London flight.

Ten days later I was back on the islands and reunited with the children, Fupi and Pinkle Purr. I found time to bring presents for the families who had taken such good care of the children and then set about writing to Elizabeth in California to explain the job offer that had come through as a result of the recent trip. It was not just the next job for me but with Claire in the top class of the primary school we had to look at the future schooling for Jonathan and Claire. If we were to continue working in developing countries then this would probably mean starting at boarding schools in England rather than risk changing schools at regular intervals as had happened during the primary school years. That first year of malnutrition had given Karoli a tough start in his development. A severe bout of measles encephalitis whilst we were in Mwanza (probably a result of his dose of measles vaccine becoming inactivated before it was administered in the days before we tightened up on the 'cold chain') had further delayed his development and progress. So Karoli would probably continue with local schooling wherever we were based.

There was a unanimous decision that we would not leave a loving dog behind again so the children insisted that Fupi would be included in any plans. Each day after school, as the sun lost its intense heat, we would take the short walk (in swimming costumes) down the hill to the shore of the lagoon. The warm shallow water was ideal for family swimming out to the small island some 400 yards from the shore. If anyone needed a rest then feet could just about touch the sandy bottom. Anyone, that is, except Fupi who always joined in the swim with great excitement. If Fupi tired then she would head for the nearest shoulders and hitch a lift for a while until her claws became so uncomfortable that she was ditched.

I had joined a madrigal group which met twice a week and (to the relief of the expatriate community) gave only very occasional performances, usually over Christmas. This group was guided by Grace, a lovely old-fashioned music teacher at the British secondary school, and as Jonathan showed an aptitude for singing he was booked in with Grace twice a week for voice training and singing lessons. A bargain was then struck that if Jonathan persisted with these lessons (often at the expense of cricket and football, which for him were a really essential part of school) to the point that were he to gain a choral scholarship at his intended preparatory school in England, then we would pay the fare and any quarantine costs for Fupi to follow the family. Thereafter Jonathan received great encouragement from all the family to attend his singing lessons each week.

Just as we were considering all the changes for the future, right out of the blue a letter arrived from friends whom we had known since university days. Sandra and Ivan both worked for the BBC and had a small house in West London where they had lived for many years. With the arrival of children they had found a small cottage on the Somerset levels to which they escaped for most weekends and school holidays. We had visited them there on several occasions when we were on leave and loved the small, quiet village and the position of their house next to the village store and post office. A compact garden ran down to the small river and the property was surrounded by green fields and occasional large herds of dairy cattle. Sandra wrote to let us know that Ivan was taking early retirement and, as she worked freelance, they intended to live in Somerset and travel to work. They had found an old Georgian pile in need of some repair a few miles away from the cottage and now they would have to sell both the town house and the cottage. If we were interested in buying the Somerset property then we could acquire it at its valuation price and they would include carpets, curtains and any furniture that we wanted. I did not have to think twice about the property offer. The cottage was ideal as a small base in a beautiful part of England at not too great a distance from Heathrow. The small village and good neighbours made for a low security risk during prolonged absences and I was all for clinching the deal as soon as possible.

The word from California was not so positive. Elizabeth had grave reservations about purchasing a property in England, even though it was planned to send Claire and Jonathan to school there. She had no wish to live in England again and viewed property as a tie to which one was compelled to return. We agreed to differ and I approached my bank for mortgage facilities and confirmed with Sandra and Ivan that we were keen to purchase.

During our last month in the New Hebrides we were treated to several 'farewell barbecues' both on the beaches at the weekends by the New Hebridean staff – coupled with sessions of beach volleyball – and in various gardens in the evening. Elizabeth had rejoined us after completing her course in the States and the packing cases were delivered to the house. The plan was to travel back to England via Bali, for a holiday, and then to settle Claire and Jonathan into schools before starting the new Tanzanian project. Arrangements were made to board Fupi with friends for three months after which she would fly to Dar es Salaam via Paris; this route meant that quarantine was not required as she was travelling to Europe via Noumea and not Australia.

We arrived back in England in August 1978, and for the very first time since leaving England we had a house of our own; we all devoted many hours to exploring the countryside and getting to know the local people and tradesmen. The acquisition of some second-hand bicycles meant that we could all explore the lanes and surrounding villages. The experience of blackberries and English apples was a most welcome delight and Jonathan was thrilled to learn that he had been awarded the choral scholarship to his preparatory school so Fupi's future with us was assured.

Through a series of letters and phone calls the nature of the Tanzanian project became clearer. In the years before independence in 1975, Mozambique had received a great deal of military assistance across its border with Tanzania, supported by Chinese military advisers. When we were living in Mwanza the southern regions of Tanzania were thus very sensitive and virtually closed to Europeans. It was at this time that many Chinese workers were in Tanzania, charged with the building of the railway from landlocked Zambia to the Indian Ocean port of Dar es Salaam. With the completion of the railway and the easing of cross-border hostilities the government of Tanzania realised that the southern regions were in need of capital investment, particularly in upgrading the roads and improving health services. When Jim Callaghan took over the reins as Prime Minister in April 1976 he lost little time in appointing Judith Hart as Minister of Overseas Development. With President Julius Nyerere demonstrating a stable (and relatively corrupt-free) socialist administration the new government agreed to a large aid programme for the southern regions of Tanzania. The initial communications between the High Commissioner and the Minister of Health in Dar es Salaam had thrown up my name in connection with the Oxfam-supported regional maternal and child health programme in Mwanza that had been such a success.

I was asked to spend two or three days each week attending meetings in London during those months of August and September to learn more of the project that was being planned. After the first of these meetings Murray asked me to bring him some genuine Somerset cider the following week. A visit to one of the local farms across the fields brought me to the source of an award-winning scrumpy, and I filled up a large plastic container that held about four litres of amber nectar. The following Monday morning I called into Murray's office on my way to be interviewed for security clearance. This was called personal vetting or PV'ed (which has quite a different connotation medically), and involved a long trawl through one's education, work experience along with exhaustive questions about family members. Murray was out and his secretary suggested that I leave the gift on his desk and he would collect it later. My day finished with a satisfactory security clearance after which I was asked to sign the Official Secrets Act. Before heading off to my hotel I called in to see Murray and confirm the timetable for the meetings the following day.

'Hope you received the scrumpy all right, Murray, I left it on the edge of your desk.'

'Thank you, Richard, so that I will not forget to take it home with me this evening, I have left it over there by my coat,' he said, gesturing towards the coat stand. A fluid-filled plastic container stood there, but it was not the plastic bottle that I had brought up.

'I'm sorry, Murray, but that's a different container. Perhaps you have decanted it!'

At this point Murray's secretary came in, having heard the exchange from her office next door.

'Oh dear!' she said. 'I think there has been a mix-up. The High Commissioner to Nigeria called in this morning and left his twenty-four-hour urine specimen that you requested.'

This long-suffering diplomat had returned for a medical assessment of his condition and had brought in his specimen as requested. Murray had sent the cider by courier to the Hospital for Tropical Diseases, and realising the mistake he immediately telephoned the laboratory there to stop them wasting his precious scrumpy. More importantly, he did not take the urine specimen back for the dinner party at home.

My trip from the New Hebrides had involved a week's visit to Tanzania after the two days of meetings in London. Murray and I were joined by Eric, an Architectural Adviser, as the central part of the project was the provision of a new teaching hospital to serve the southern regions of Tanzania. In addition the project would involve the provision of six new rural health centres and enhanced support for the national tuberculosis and leprosy programme, mainly in the form of microscopes and transport. Joined by the first secretary from the British High Commission, we attended meetings at the Ministry of Health in Dar es Salaam to try a reach a decision on where the new hospital should be sited. The two options were Mtwara, a town on the coast in the south-east of the country, or Mbeya, a highland town in the far south-west close to the Zambian border, and plans were made for us to visit each site.

A twin-engined Cessna was our means of transport for the internal flights in Tanzania and we were accompanied by the first secretary from the High Commission on each of the day trips, with Mtwara being the first site. We flew due south out of Dar very early in the morning, and after about thirty minutes we sighted the great Rufiji River delta, with the island of Mafia out on the horizon opposite the river mouth. It was in this mangrove-lined river that the *Königsberg*, a large German battleship, was scuttled in 1916 during the First World War. The resourceful commanding officer of the German forces, Von Lettow, organised the removal of the huge guns from the ship and manhandled them across vast areas of southern Tanzania, using them with devastating effect in battle. From our small cockpit we were unable to see any sign of the hulk of the ship which was probably too far up the river.

Mtwara town was smaller than we had expected with a very quiet port, and many of the buildings and facilities were run down. Eric very quickly assessed that if we were to choose Mtwara as the site of the new hospital then all the heavy goods and building materials would have to be shipped through the port at Dar es Salaam rather than Mtwara. The Regional Commissioner and his team met us at the airport and drove us to their headquarters where we listened to their suggestions on the siting of the hospital. They were looking at a flat site not far from the town, defending this suggestion by pointing out that no new development had taken place in Mtwara since the end of the German occupation.

The Regional Commissioner explained that in the days before the start of the First World War the German district officer sited his headquarters on the top of a local hill as this location was perceived to be healthier, with lower humidity and fewer mosquitoes. The local people had access to the district commissioner at 5 p.m. each evening to present their problems and in Swahili he was referred to as '*Bwana Shauri*' – the problem man. The trouble was that the hill was so steep that by the time the locals reached the DC's office they were so out of breath that they could barely speak. The German DC ran his office with such efficiency that every complainant was seen promptly as soon as they arrived, so the result of this extreme exercise was that the daily session was very short. Ever since that part of their history the people of Mtwara had avoided new buildings on hills.

We had a day in Dar es Salaam after this trip for detailed discussions before heading off to the far south-west and the town of Mbeya. As with any highland area in East Africa, the climate is much more to the liking of Europeans than the hot, humid coastal strip, and as we flew into the town in the early morning there was a low mist covering all the houses whilst the surrounding hill peaks stood out proudly in the strong sun. We were again met by the Regional Commissioner and his party, which included, to my great surprise, Helena, who had been matron at the teaching hospital in Mwanza when I had left Tanzania two years previously. Her husband, a well-respected lawyer, had decided to move the family back to their home area of Mbeya now that all the foreign troops had moved out of the area and the High Court of Tanzania had reopened in the town. Helena had just started work at the hospital in Mbeya and had seen my name on the information sheet of the visiting party and guessed that I had come back to Tanzania. She gave me an effusive, almost embarrassing, welcome.

The proposed site in Mbeya was essentially the existing hospital campus where there was room to develop a new hospital with minimum disturbance to the daily routine. After a detailed tour we repaired to the Mbeya Railway Hotel for lunch, where old-fashioned standards were still maintained. Double damask, freshly laundered table linen; Sheffield plate condiment sets, white earthenware East African Railways crockery and a first course of brown Windsor soup.

Our return flight to Dar was a little eventful as the pilot indicated that a large tropical storm lay right in our flight path. As we were not pressurised we could not fly above it, and so there was no alternative but to make a detour and fly through the fringes. Even this plan proved to be very lumpy, with huge flashes of lightning to the port side. All conversation ceased until we were safely through the worst. The pilot then informed us that the last time he had flown through such a storm (two weeks earlier in the Kenyan Rift Valley) one early flash of lightning had damaged the compass so badly that by the time they came through the upheaval he really had no idea of his bearings. Seeing a main road, they dropped down and flew above the road until they came to a crossroads with a signpost. He asked the passengers to look out of the window as they circled round in order to confirm the direction of Nairobi.

We were all relieved to have made it to Dar without problems, only for the pilot to inform us that there was a hitch with the landing gear. He thought that the wheels had come down ready for landing but a light on his panel indicated that they were still retracted. He would have to fly past the control tower two or three times and seek their opinion. Fortunately after only a couple of circles we were informed that the wheels were down and we came in to land just hoping that they were correctly locked in that position.

Further discussions at the Ministry of Health allowed us to finalise the plan for locating the new hospital in Mbeya, whilst the construction of six new rural health centres, along with new Land Rover ambulances, would be concentrated in the Mtwara and Lindi regions in the south east. The next step was to recruit a team of experienced expatriate personnel who would form the nucleus for planning, costing and implementing the project. I was certain that John, our hospital secretary in Mwanza, had handled himself responsibly and given a good account of himself to the Tanzanian Ministry of Health during the six years that he had worked there. I had the address of his mother in Dorset and made contact to see if he could be persuaded to join the team, along with Barbara, his wife, whose expertise in hospital laboratory work would be invaluable. Richard, the district medical officer based at Tanna in the New Hebrides, had worked in leprosy and tuberculosis in Zambia before going out to the Pacific islands and would be ideal in that role of the project. Elizabeth, with her recently acquired qualification and her previous work in the Mwanza maternal and child health programme, should be viewed as a suitable candidate by the Tanzanian government to implement the aid being directed towards new rural health centres.

At this very early stage of planning I became aware of the rules of the game with inter-government aid programmes. The donor agency would attempt to ensure that the maximum amount of the material goods involved in the building of a capital project would be provided by the country donating the aid. So with this project all the hospital beds, furniture, sterilisers and operating-theatre equipment would be made in England and would be ordered through the Crown Agents. Even the cement and reinforced steel for the buildings would be exported out to Tanzania. The recipient country held a veto over any staff member of the project team who was considered unsuitable, either by way of qualifications, experience or political affiliation. Interestingly, there was already a Briton in post there.

During our short visit to Mbeya and the renewal of my friendship with Helena, she told me of a British physician who had been working at the government hospital in Mbeya for the past ten years. Nigel was very highly thought of by the local community and had been able to continue working in Mbeya through the long period of political sensitivity simply because he was the traditional eccentric Englishman. Thoroughly forgetful about all matters unrelated to his work and totally devoted to his patients, he was never viewed as a political risk and continued to work in the southern highlands at a time when all other Europeans were carefully vetted. His mode of dress was eccentric Edwardian, and Helena informed me that he was famous for always reporting to the police that his aged Peugeot had been stolen on the odd occasion when he went into town shopping. The fact that Nigel would come out of the shop and totally forget where he had parked the vehicle was well known to the police. Certain officers were delegated to watch out for the car in the town in order to shorten the search process. In recognition of his vast amount of local experience and knowledge it was suggested that Nigel's contract should be changed in order to offer him similar terms to other British team members. Nigel was delighted and immediately ordered a new car on the strength of these expectations.

During the autumn of 1978 we settled Claire and Jonathan into their new schools and then flew out with Karoli to meet up with Fupi and to set up an office and a working base in Dar es Salaam. We understood that it would be some months before we moved to Mbeya, and in the meantime I was attached to the High Commission to work closely with the first secretary on the first stages of the project. We had no house, and rental of suitable property in the capital was difficult, almost impossible. We had to rely on 'house warming' for High Commission staff who were on leave, which proved to be an unsettling process for all concerned, moving house every six to eight weeks. There were times when none of the High Commission staff was on leave and we then depended on the kindness of a bachelor diplomat to open his large house and accommodate our family for a few weeks. As I was still on the Tanzanian medical register the Deputy High Commissioner suggested that I might act as medical officer to the High

Commission staff and their families. It was not strictly in the job description, but realising that housing our family whilst we were temporarily based in Dar depended on the goodwill of the Foreign Office staff, I readily agreed. Murray, who was powerless to resolve the housing problem, encouraged me, insisting that 'A little bit of general practice never did anyone any harm.'

The commonest problem at that time was the level of depression amongst the wives of the diplomats with children of school age. The obligation to send the children off to boarding schools in the UK meant that the mothers were locked into a small community in a large sprawling city with high temperatures and humidity. Life only took on any meaning during the school holidays and quite often their husband's duties took them away up country for several days or even weeks at a time. One such wife had been seeing me for treatment for her depression and insomnia, and she seemed to be making good progress until her husband had to go off to work in Zanzibar for a week. The day after his departure the houseboy, who had been with them for some time, came to see her.

'Madam,' he said very quietly, 'I must ask for a few days' leave as I have just heard that my father has died and I must bury him.'

'Well, of course, Abdul,' she replied. 'You must leave at once, and as my husband is away this week there is no entertaining, so take the rest of this week off.'

'Thank you, madam, but I also have one great problem.'

'Yes. What is that?'

'I need a suit, madam, so could you advance me some money and I can purchase one today.'

'I have a better idea,' the lady of the house replied. 'You are about the same size as my husband, so why don't you borrow one of his suits and that will mean that you can go straight home for the funeral.'

'You are very kind.'

Without further ado she rummaged through her husband's wardrobe and found a very respectable dark suit ideal for the occasion. Abdul went off with the folded suit under his arm and she contented herself knowing that she would have time to get it cleaned and returned to the wardrobe before her husband was even aware of its absence. Four days later Abdul returned from his family home.

'Did everything go well with the funeral, Abdul?'

'Oh yes, madam, it was a lovely occasion and all the family were there together. They asked me to thank you as my father looked so nice in your husband's suit.'

I advised the distressed lady to inform her husband of these events as soon as a suitable opportunity presented rather that bottle up the guilty secret and make her depression even worse.

In May 1979 the general election brought Mrs Thatcher and a conservative government into power. Lord Carrington was appointed as Foreign Secretary, and the Ministry of Overseas Development was abolished and incorporated into the Foreign and Commonwealth Office. At first the ripples of these changes made little impact with us as all attention was focused on the need to resolve Ian Smith and the Rhodesia problem. To this end Lord Carrington made several visits to the 'front-line states', particularly Zambia and Tanzania, before the Lancaster House Conference was called to resolve the issues and create the independent country of Zimbabwe. In order to give the seal of approval to these negotiations a royal visit to Tanzania, Malawi, Botswana and Zambia was planned for the end of July. I was approached by the High Commissioner and asked if I would offer my services to the royal party as the local doctor. One of the royal surgeons would be travelling with the party from London, but I would liaise with him beforehand and accompany him during the three days of the visit in case there was a need for hospital care.

Dar es Salaam presented no problem, as I knew all the senior medical staff in the University Teaching Hospital, but the planned day in Zanzibar was an unknown quantity. I was informed that a very efficient Chinese medical team ran the hospital on the island, but as to what facilities were available no one at the Ministry had any idea of the standard of services or specialities of the doctors. I had to fly over to Zanzibar for a day and diplomatically find out as much as I could about the availability of various drugs and emergency equipment.

Zanzibar was even more ramshackle and run-down than the poorer areas of Dar es Salaam, but the elegant Arab architecture and style were still very much in evidence. Wonderful tall carved, brass-studded hardwood doors opened into small dusty courtyards from which the crumbling paintwork and wooden filigree balconies of a group of family homes could be made out.

In January 1964 some forty men, led by John Okello, crawled through the wire surrounding the Zurani police barracks in Zanzibar at three o'clock in the morning and overpowered the two armed sentries on guard. All the other police were sleeping upstairs to keep cool, so the rebels were able to break into the armoury and help themselves to rifles and ammunition. There followed one of the fastest coups in African history, and by noon of that same day the hereditary Sultan, whose family had ruled the islands for over 130 years, had fled with his entourage. As these two small islands of Zanzibar and Pemba were economically vulnerable, the new Republic of Tanganyika agreed to merge to form the Republic of Tanzania in 1964.

Both these islands had grown cloves and other spices commercially for many years, and during my assessment visit I was taken to see a clove estate, which happened to be next door to an old leprosarium. This was still functioning and catering for a dozen or more patients in buildings that had changed little since they were erected at the turn of the last century. Close to the sea and with high ceilings and huge open (but netted) windows, it probably presented an ideal location and environment for the treatment and rehabilitation of these poor patients.

On the day of the royal visit I was flown out from Dar, along with many other officials, about thirty minutes ahead of the royal flight. The royal surgeon accompanying the party and myself were allocated Number Eight car in the motorcade. The first three cars were pristine black Mercedes and Tim, one of the diplomats travelling with us, had the small royal standard in his pocket that would be affixed to the leading car. Our vehicle was a slightly dusty and well-travelled Mercedes, but after Number Ten the cars became less prestigious and by the time Number Twenty was reached they were down to Land Rovers.

The Queen and the Duke would make a tour of the town, stopping by the old administrative centre for a walkabout for approximately thirty minutes. A series of speeches would then follow, with introductions to the officials in the Zanzibar party, before a slow drive back to the airport. Whilst most of the route was over a reasonable two-lane road, in the old town of Zanzibar the buildings formed the road edges; wide cars had never been considered in the original design of these narrow alleyways. Thus there really was no space at times for two vehicles to pass each other in comfort.

All went well with the motorcade until we entered the old part of the town, and after a few minutes our driver commented in Swahili: 'I can only see one car behind us now. Perhaps there has been a breakdown.'

'I think we follow the same route going back,' I volunteered to him, 'so perhaps there will be a real mess when the two parts of the motorcade meet head on.'

'You are right, Daktari, you should mention this to your boss when we stop.'

Shortly after this we arrived at the old administrative building, which was situated very close to the sea front. Whilst the Queen and the Duke walked among the small crowd that had gathered, I took the opportunity to speak with Tim and explained that less than half of the motorcade that had started had actually made it to this point. He alerted his Zanzibari counterpart and they decided to extend the proceedings until we were certain that the return route to the airport was clear. During this interval the Duke of Edinburgh pulled out what appeared to be a gold-plated pocket camera and took a series of photos for the family album. To our great relief car Number Eleven hove into view, tightly packed with the occupants of the broken-down vehicle (which had been abandoned) plus the original complement, so we were free to set off back to the airport.

The only calls on my medical services during the three-day state visit involved attention to a distressed lady-in-waiting, who had woken to find a rat running across the foot of her bed in the hotel, and to reassure the assistant captain of the royal flight that his ingrowing toenail would not prevent him from flying on to Malawi the following day.

Once the Rhodesia situation had been settled and the royal visit was over, the High Commissioner departed for a few weeks of leave and, with Claire and Jonathan out in Tanzania for the long summer school holidays, we looked at some leave as well. We had no accommodation available at that time in Dar es Salaam, so we decided to go back to the safari tent and visit one of the two large game reserves in the south of Tanzania. The Selous, the largest game reserve in Africa, is in the south-east of the country, covering a vast area of 25,000 square kilometres, and runs from the Rufiji River almost to the Mozambique border. The Ruaha, roughly the same size as the Serengeti, is situated more centrally in the southern regions, occupying a tract of land between the Great Ruaha River and the upper reaches of the Rufiji River. As we could arrange to do some work in Mbeya on either side of the holiday, we opted for a trip to the Ruaha.

We realised that no food or drink was going to be available within the reserve so, stopping at the town of Iringa, we loaded up with vegetables and fresh fruit, and amongst the latter were included some of the small juicy orange-skinned mangoes that were in season at the time. After a long drive, in the course of which we saw both greater and lesser kudu for the first time, we finally arrived at the campsite on the banks of the Great Ruaha River. Whilst we set up camp the children were allowed to tuck into the mangoes for the first time; mango juice on small fingers in a tightly packed Land Rover is an evil combination. Most of the small mangoes were eaten with decorum close to the tent with a bucket of water handy to wash the hands and face after each assault.

Jonathan chose to consume his portion of the fruit whilst stretching his legs by wandering round the campsite. Dusk was approaching as we sat around the campfire and started to cook the supper when, seemingly out of nowhere, a huge lone bull elephant approached the campsite. We all moved quickly into the mosquito-netted verandah as the safety of the Land Rover was a good few steps away and watched anxiously. The tip of the elephant's trunk was working ceaselessly and then it latched upon the scent that had attracted it to the campsite – Jonathan's discarded mango skins. Carefully, this huge creature walked around the tent, raising its feet very delicately over the guy ropes, to pick up each of the discarded skins. Claire was both frightened and a bit irritated.

'How many mangoes did you eat and where did you go to eat them all?' she asked Jonathan, who was fast collecting the blame for a delayed supper.

Eventually the solitary bull had tracked down all of the delicacies and wandered off to the river for a good wallow whilst we salvaged a late supper. The following three days we followed many game routes through this wild and natural reserve, seeing lion, cheetah and leopard in addition to the large herds of elephant for which this vast area is famous. We came across three rangers at the Ruaha River office, who gave us information and a guide leaflet about the hugely varied bird population in the reserve, especially in the vicinity of the river; they also confirmed that we were the only visitors in the Ruaha at that time. Even today this reserve is so inaccessible that few visitors make the effort to visit the area, and the wildlife remains totally natural.

During the time that we were working in Mbeya we became aware of rumours that the whole aid programme was being cut back. On returning to Dar es Salaam it was confirmed that in the space of eighteen months the British government had altered its view, and no longer held socialist Tanzania in the same rosy glow. The hospital was now to be a rebuild of the existing poor and decrepit facilities in Mbeya; the programme of building rural health centres in the southern regions was to be reduced and the financial support for the national TB and leprosy programme was to be cut back. Word quickly spread to the regional office in Mbeya that the British government was not offering a new hospital, only a refurbishment, so the local politicians decided to 'cold shoulder' the team members in the mistaken belief that their opposition to this new plan would persuade Mrs Thatcher to make a full reinstatement of the original undertaking. Little did they or we appreciate the unshakeable resolve of this lady at that time.

Two months later we were heartened to read that the consignment of twenty new Land Rovers destined for the national TB and leprosy programme (that had been ordered before the change in government) was in a vessel on the 'outer anchorage' and should be at the docks with a few days. This national programme had been running for many years with medication provided by the WHO, but the constant problem of follow-up to ensure compliance with medication and contact tracing in the rural communities depended on dependable transport. Perhaps this tangible part of the original project might improve the soured relations with the Tanzanian Ministry officials, particularly as Land Rover enjoy a reputation second to none throughout East Africa as a reliable workhorse that can get through the most adverse conditions. In addition there was a provision of twenty-five Land Rover ambulance conversions for the rural areas of Mtwara and Lindi.

At that time all other donor countries took full responsibility for port clearing and onward forwarding of all equipment coming through Dar es Salaam Port. Only the British government and the UN agencies used the government central medical stores as their agent for handling and forwarding, possibly out of a fear of being branded as neo-colonialist. The sad result was that three months after unloading only nine of the forty-five vehicles had reached their up-country destinations. The remainder had been so badly pilfered either in the port area or in the central medical stores compound that being without batteries, carburettors or solenoid switches they were lying idle whilst the Ministry of Health found funds and placed orders with Land Rover in England for replacement parts.

As we approached the new year of 1980 I wrote my annual report on the progress of the project after the first full year, expressing concern at the way in which the original programme had been so heavily cut back. I also emphasised that the Tanzanian response, both in Mbeya and in Dar, had understandably been one of poor communication and co-operation. His Excellency was not at all pleased with my report and I was summoned to his office. There I was informed that the British Diplomatic Service enjoyed a long tradition of drafting reports and communications that were measured, understated and free from personal opinions. He advised me to study the official reports sent to the Admiralty during and after the Battle of Jutland if the opportunity ever presented itself to me.

I communicated to Murray in London that the diplomatic role did not sit easily with me and that I would move down to Mbeya, putting 800 miles between myself and the offices of the High

Commission. Hopefully I would be able to find some clinical work by operating on some of the more complex gynaecological problems in the local district and mission hospitals to build up some local contacts and confidence. Between us we also organised a flying visit from an eye surgeon friend of mine in Bath who would undertake cataract surgery under local anaesthetic at district hospitals in the area. Robin had undertaken similar work in southern Africa and so was able to draw up a list of instruments for procurement through the Crown Agents, along with a good supply of robust spectacles. These were the days before lens implants, and the operation simply involved the removal of the opaque lens from the eye.

During a three-week visit Robin ran morning clinics to select suitable patients from the long lines of nearly blind patients who had been assembled by the medical officer and his staff outside the hospital. Having trained me to give the local anaesthetic, Robin then set to work on an operating list around noon. By late afternoon, when we were finishing, the first few elderly patients on the list were just leaving for home, having had their eye bandages removed. Their squeals of delight at being able to see again were clearly audible to us through the open windows of the operating theatre.

Richard's enthusiastic efforts with the TB and leprosy programme were appreciated and he seemed settled in a small house on the fringe of the old hospital compound. Barbara and John had also settled in well and were making some headway in persuading the local government officials to accept the new scaled-down programme for the Mbeya Hospital.

The laboratory staff New Year's party had ended in tragedy when two of the local laboratory technicians failed to report for work the following morning. When roused they indicated that they must have overslept but, strangely, they thought it was still dark. Some of the party drinks had been enhanced by alcohol smuggled out of the laboratory, but this was methyl alcohol, and these two young men, whose drinks had been heavily laced, were now permanently blinded as a result.

Being at altitude in Africa is always a special experience, whether it is the Atlas Mountains in Morocco, the foothills and slopes of Kilimanjaro or the Ruwenzori Mountains in Uganda. Mbeya was no exception and climbing the peak at the far end of the old hospital compound not only afforded a panoramic view of the township and suburbs below but also gave the opportunity to walk for miles on the grassy uplands above the town. Here pale yellow *helichrysum* grew wild, along with tall elegant pink wind flowers, and black kites soared high in the thermals. It was here, whilst walking, that we met Father Phil, a White Father in charge of a large parish just south of Mbeya. Phil hailed from Lancashire but had spent more than twenty years in the southern highlands, and was an enthusiastic botanist, ornithologist and conservationist. He was delighted to find English people with similar interests and he took us on many walks and rambles, identifying all the flowers and birds with a Franciscan love and intensity, and he often used to call into one of the project quarters in the evening for a meal and a chat.

During the Easter school holidays the children enjoyed many of his conducted walks over the weekends, but it became obvious that both Claire and Jonathan were not happy at boarding school. Communications from Mbeya were very difficult, with letters taking more than a week to reach England and unreliable telephone connections only possible between 11 a.m. and 6 p.m. I had to return to London for meetings in mid-April and it was agreed that I should fly back with Claire and Jonathan and see them back into their schools. I had lost much of my initial commitment and enthusiasm for the now scaled-down project, finding it difficult to reconcile the needs of such a poor country with a huge reduction in an agreed aid programme. But I also realised that I was there as a civil servant of the British government. Elizabeth indicated that she wished to continue working on the project for the remaining year of her contract, whilst I had a wish to return to clinical medicine and also to be near to Claire and Jonathan in England. Having settled the two of them in school for the summer term (and hitting freak snow conditions in Somerset at the end of April) I met up with Murray in London and tendered my resignation as Project Co-ordinator.

I returned to Tanzania to work out my three months' notice and immediately explained the reasons behind my decision to terminate my contract to Bob and his colleagues at the High Commission. During my final weeks in Tanzania I joined Phil on one of his walks. He seemed to understand all the reasons behind my decision.

'I'm blessed that I am able to work amongst wonderful people in my parish, tucked away in a remote corner of the country. Nobody interferes with me or tells me what to do or when to do it.' He tied up his stout walking boots, stretched his thin legs and pushed his glasses up on the bridge of his nose.

'Let's go for a walk in primary rainforest and look at the canopy.'

We drove for half an hour south from his mission along a rugged road, and the forest gradually closed in upon us until we stopped at a small clearing. Grabbing his stout stick from the back of the Land Rover we walked into the gloom of this thick forest, and after ten minutes he stopped and looked up.

'There you are,' he said, pointing upwards.

Following the direction of his finger I saw a group of long-haired black and white Colobus monkeys leaping around the canopy of this unspoilt section of tropical forest.

'Magic!' said Phil.

Two weeks later I was back in England for the start of the school summer holidays and applying for a position to train as a general practitioner at my local surgery in Somerset with Fupi in quarantine kennels some ten miles away.

Printed in the United Kingdom
by Lightning Source UK Ltd.
113192UKS00001B/73